ANGLO-SAXON ABOLITION

OF

NEGRO SLAVERY.

BY

F. W: NEWMAN, M.R.A.S.,

EMERITUS PROFESSOR OF UNIVERSITY COLLEGE, LONDON,

ONCE FELLOW OF BALLIOL COLLEGE, OXFORD.

HONORARY FELLOW OF WORCESTER COLLEGE, OXFORD.

NEGRO UNIVERSITIES PRESS
NEW YORK

ERRATA.

In p. 1, last line, *for* Quasher *read* Quashee.
In p 106, line 5, *for* four millions *read* three millions.

Originally published in 1889
by Kegan Paul, Trench & Co., London

Reprinted 1969 by
Negro Universities Press
A DIVISION OF GREENWOOD PUBLISHING CORP.
NEW YORK

SBN 8371-1643-0

PRINTED IN UNITED STATES OF AMERICA

CONTENTS.

———

PART I.

ERRATA.

Page 22, line 15, for "had all" read "had on all."

Page 31, line 10, for "has been" read "had been."

Page 35, line 24, for "Whigs" read "to Whigs."

Page 38, line 1, for "in England" read "under England."

Page 43, line 19, for "successful" read "rightful."

Page 71, here and elsewhere, for "F. C. Adams" replace "C. F. Adams."

Page 72, line 18, for "epithets are not" read "these epithets are."

Page 74, line 23, for "system" read "question."

Page 76, line 5, for "President Monroe" read "President Madison."

Page 78, line 19, for "sometime" read "sometimes."

Page 82, line 12, for "Royal Arbitration" read "Court of Arbitration."
   Also line 21, after "I understand" add "nay, the Minister.
   Mr. C. F. Adams."

Page 85, line 11, for "level" read "local."

Page 87. I now learn that Stonewall Jackson was never Commander-
   in-Chief, and that he was slain in Virginia.—F. W. N.

Page 98, line 5, for "in which" read "on which."

PART I.

NEGRO SLAVERY UNDER ENGLISH RULE.

From "FRAZER'S MAGAZINE," January, 1879.

ABUNDANT experience has established in the cultivated men of Europe, as testified in European literature, the conviction that a fixed system of slavery is a deadly plague-spot in any national institution. Notoriously, it is fatally demoralizing to the masters, and inevitably oppressive to the slaves. From an industrial aspect it is intensely wasteful; and by dishonouring labour, it propagates idleness and vice among poor freemen. Through the danger of insurrections it also conduces to military weakness. Notwithstanding the attempts in the American Union at a philosophic defence of the cruel and ruinous system but lately dominant there, and the deplorable support given to them in England by *one eminent man of letters*,* we can happily say that the vile and hateful institution is now thoroughly condemned by the collective European intellect.

But unhappily English colonists and seamen in large numbers are unversed in our higher literature, are

---

* I am asked, what eminent man of letters is alluded to, as in England foremost in defence of slavery. Younger readers who cannot remember, have a right to be informed. It alludes to Thomas Carlyle, author of a *History of the French Revolution*, which first made him famous and popular. Even in it his too great admiration of mere strength of character was painfully indicated by his warm sentiment for Danton; but afterwards flamed out in fatuous scorn against *Black Quasher* and English *Bobus*, of which the less said, the better.

ignorant of past history, and, when out of reach of
English law, are very apt to reconstruct both law and
morals for themselves. In many of our colonies, as in
the Mauritius and in Queensland, local laws are made
which reduce Chinese immigrants to a state closely similar
to slavery. In the English West Indies nothing but the
strong hand of the Home Government stops the importation of coolies to be converted into virtual slaves; and
the temper shown by the whites of the Cape Colony
towards the native Kafirs and Hottentots is anything but
reassuring. It is but a little while ago since the excellent
and humane Commodore Goodenough was killed on one
island of the Pacific, and Bishop Patteson on another,
because English merchant ships had carried natives away
by fraud or violence. Fiji has narrowly been rescued
from such lawless treatment, and Sir Arthur Gordon, the
governor, without very ample and exceptional powers,
would be quite unable to suppress our buccaneers, who
with the arts of high civilization and the enterprize of
capital unite gross and heartless brutality. Unless knowledge in the English public reinforce our Government,
which is always so overworked as to lean towards evil
laxity, the British colonies are likely to use their early
freedom in this pernicious direction. But (so many are
the novelties and distractions of English politics) our
young people in tens of thousands are totally ignorant
of the history of negro slavery. Even those who cannot
at all be called uneducated easily believe bold assertions
—such as, that the liberation of West Indian slaves was
an unfortunate mistake and a failure; that the anti-
slavery party ought to have aimed at gradual abolition
and did not; that they were fanatics; that the islands
have never been so prosperous since the emancipation;
and that as slaves the blacks were better off and better
behaved than now. So widespread is ignorance of this

great and melancholy history in the younger generation, that it is believed a retrospect in moderate compass may be timely and acceptable.

The first matter perhaps on which a distinct understanding is desirable, is the legal aspect of the slave trade and of slavery. The one and the other were from the beginning utterly illegal, and only gained a show of legality through the malversations and neglects of *Executive* officers, whose real duty was to denounce the system and suppress it wherever it lay in their power. The position of the English king and his chief ministers was in early days somewhat difficult, and a few words may be not amiss on this head. The power of Queen Elizabeth by sea was very puny in comparison to that of Spain; the supplies of her exchequer scant. She rejoiced in the exploits of individual sea-captains, with little inquiry as to the legality of their proceedings, whether towards Spaniards or Africans. The English slave trade, in fact, began with Sir John Hawkins in the year 1562. He had obtained leave from the Queen to carry Africans to America *with their own free consent;* but he forced them on board his ships not without slaughter, and escaped without punishment; nay, a few years later, received high honour from the Queen. When Virginia attained a fixed condition as a colony—scarcely before 1615, in which year fifty acres of land were assigned to every emigrant and his heirs—the cultivation of tobacco instantly followed. Five years later a Dutch ship brought a cargo of negroes from the coast of Africa, whom the Virginians (a mixed body of very low morals) joyfully received as slaves. But neither the slave trade nor slavery had any legal sanction. King James was always in debt, and far too much occupied with his own miserable pleasures to care about such a peccadillo, though in granting a new constitution for Virginia he reserved a veto to their laws for the Court in England. Under James I. and Charles I. the English Parliament was helpless, and the slavery once introduced became chronic; children and grandchildren were born in slavery, and the system spread to our other colonies on the Continent. Of the West Indian islands, most were occupied, and slavery introduced, by other European nations before us, so that England, in conquering them, found slavery existing.

No sooner had we got free from struggle against the Stuarts, than King William III. involved us in Continental war. Our growing maritime power sufficed to enforce anything upon the colonies on which the Parliament was bent; but the mass of the people knew little about the negroes, and the religion of Protestants, being constructed too much on the mere letter of the Bible, was not at all shocked by the idea of slavery. It was otherwise with the slave *trade*. Man-stealing is denounced by name in the New Testament as an odious wickedness, and common sense taught everyone that to hunt and capture Africans for slaves or to buy them of the captors was as gross and indefensible a cruelty as if Algerines were to land on our coasts and carry Englishmen into slavery—a lot which did befall some of our seamen when intercepted by these pirates. Brydges, in his *History of Jamaica*, tells us that as many as 70,000 slaves were imported into that island during the ten years 1751-60. It is a popular error to suppose that Parliament passed a law to legalise the slave trade—an error propagated by the violent and unscrupulous men who engaged in it. But the law which undertook to "regulate the trade of Africa" (23rd of George II.) added a strict prohibition, under penalties, against taking on board or carrying away any African "by force or fraud." Fraud and violence were freely used; but the colonial authorities winked at it. The Home Ministry perhaps had no "official information;" and even in this century we know that the President of the Board of Control and the Chairman of the Hon. East India Company professed in Parliament profound ignorance and disbelief of what was notorious to the missionaries and indigo planters, that the revenue over a great part of India was collected by torture. Each Ministry in turn coveted the support of as many "interests" as possible, and dreaded to make any great "interest" its enemy.

How soon "the planting interest" became powerful it is hard to say, but it is certain that in the middle of the last century they were a compact political body, and that there was a permanent connivance on the part of the British Ministries, who did not choose to risk incurring the planters' enmity. Besides, since the Crown had reserved for itself a veto on colonial legislation, which abounded with Acts assuming slavery as legal, and with severe enforcements on the oppressed victims, all the Ministries in succession implicated themselves in the guilt by not advising the Sovereign to use the veto. Moreover, as time went on, the English Crown had slave colonies of its own, in which was no Colonial Legislature. These were counted as four, viz., two in Guiana (Demerara and Berbice), St. Lucia, and Trinidad. The Cape and the Mauritius were soon added. Thus while no Parliamentary sanction was given to the slave trade or to slavery (further than the careless use of the word *slave*, perhaps by the cunning amendment of planters sitting in the House), the Executive Government both at home and in the colonies treacherously and by *lachesse* established it in fact, though this could not make it legal. Americans of the Southern States have often reproached England with "forcing slavery upon them." It is very certain that they were glad to be "forced;" but their plea suggests that some of our

Ministries went beyond connivance, and actually promoted the pernicious and horrible institution. One glaring fact may here be pointed at, as showing against what a power in Parliament itself an English Ministry had to struggle in the first quarter of this century. St. Domingo or Hayti had effected its actual liberation from France, but was often threatened by the French arms. During our many wars with France or Spain, we had zealously seized Canada and Acadia on the continent, and among islands the Mauritius, Grenada, St. Vincent, Dominica, and Trinidad, yet we rejected all the overtures of free Hayti, and would in no way acknowledge her independence. The Haytians were ready to make every concession for the advantage of our commerce and our acknowledgment; many said they would have even adopted our language; but to their earnest entreaties for friendship we replied by an Act of Parliament which prohibited all intercourse between Hayti and Jamaica! When Mr. Canning recognised the independence of Spanish America, no mention was made of Hayti, which at last was in consequence forced to compromise with France. As late as 1825 an Act was passed declaring the forfeiture of any British ship, with its cargo, which should sail from Jamaica to St. Domingo or from St. Domingo to Jamaica, and forbidding any foreign ship that had touched at St. Domingo to enter any port of Jamaica. So powerful was West Indian sentiment in both Houses of Parliament! Yet the planters never dared to try to obtain any Act that should directly legitimate slavery.

The American lawyers who wrote and spoke in the interest of the slaveholders were well aware that slavery rested on no other basis than *custom* and *local law*. Henry Clay, in 1839, summed up the argument thus: "Two hundred years of legislation have sanctified (!) and sanctioned negro slaves as property." But no early

American colony passed any enactment to *originate* the relation of master and slave; they did but *assume* the relation and make laws to secure or regulate it. No slaveholder was able to prove in court that a particular man or woman was his slave according to law. Hence Mr. Mason, of Virginia, when the Fugitive Slave Bill was pending, resisted the claim of trial by jury, because it would bring up the question of the legality of slavery, *which* (he said) *it would be impossible to prove !* On this ground, Congress struck out the jury trial !

When the question came on in the British Parliament concerning the slave trade, Mr. Pitt cited the Act (23 George II.), and insisted that it was a direct *prohibition* of the slave trade in the fact that it prohibited fraud and violence; and it gradually became impossible to hold any other view. Mr. Canning, in 1799, signalised himself by his usual eloquence, of which some sentences must be here recorded : " Trust not the masters of slaves in legislation for slavery. However specious their laws may appear, depend upon it they must be ineffectual in their operation. It is in the nature of things that they should be so. Let then the British House of Commons do their part themselves. Let them not delegate the trust of doing it to those who cannot execute that trust fairly. Let the evil be remedied by an assembly of freemen, by the Government of a free people, not the masters of slaves. Their laws can never reach the evil. There is something in the nature of absolute authority, in the relation between master and slave, which makes despotism in all cases and in all circumstances an incompetent and unsure executor even of its own provisions in favour of the objects of its power." Of course, this presumed that the masters did not wish to get rid of their despotism. Mr. Canning knew the West Indians too well. His words were sadly justified in the sequel. Yet it was not given to the Tory party to abolish even the slave trade. The West Indian interest was to them then nearly what the Publican interest is 'now. Mr. Pitt died, in January 1806, broken-hearted by the successes of Napoleon, and Lord Grenville succeeded him as Prime Minister, with Fox (ever the advocate of peace) as Foreign Secretary, who, in June, moved a resolution against the slave trade. But he was already in very bad health, and died after being in office eight months. "Two things," he said on his death-bed, "I wish to see accomplished: peace with Europe, and the abolition of the slave trade: but of the two, *I wish more the latter.*" He had to bequeath the completion of this work to his successors. Lord Grey (then Lord Howick) passed the Bill triumphantly through the Commons, and Lord Grenville with difficulty carried it to a final issue on the 25th of March, 1807, a few minutes before the Ministers resigned, disgusted with the King's obstinacy concerning the Catholics. Next year the United States declared the slave trade to be *piracy,* herein going beyond England in severity.

The agitation against the slave trade, carried on in Parliament by the eloquence of Wilberforce, and aided by the learning and zeal of many eminent talents, was a great enlightenment to England; but it was not the first step towards emancipation. A first-rate judicial sentence had already pronounced against slavery: which was the more remarkable and the more important, since English judges in general, as other civil officials, had indirectly sanctioned the institution. Under the circumstances it was to be expected. In the colonies where slavery existed, every man of importance held slaves; the income of all the educated classes depended on slavery. The very men appointed as protectors of slaves were generally slave-holders, and the judges as well as the clergy were implicated in the same interest. When the colonial lawyers and judges recognised slaves as property, and their documents were produced in an English court, where no advocate stood up to protest in the interest of the blacks that men and women were not and could not be property, no one could expect an English judge to open this question of himself. As he could not effect the freedom of the human beings called "property," he would seem to himself to be injuring a white person with no benefit to the blacks. In the result the slave-owners were able to claim that their right of property in slaves had been again and again acknowledged by English judges. Yet, as hinted above, a critical case had already occurred, which deserves here special detail.

A planter brought to London a slave called James Somerset, in 1772, and when he fell ill, inhumanly turned him out of doors. Mr. Granville Sharp, a philanthropic barrister, found him in the street, placed him in a hospital where he recovered his health, and then got him a situation as a servant. Two years after, his old master arrested and imprisoned him as a runaway slave. Mr. Sharp brought the case before the Lord Mayor, who ordered Somerset to be set at liberty. But the master seized him violently in presence of the Lord Mayor and Mr. Sharp; on which the latter brought an action against the master for assault. The question of law was finally referred to the twelve judges, in February and May of that year, who decided *unanimously*, that no man can be accounted a slave on English territory. This decision is often quoted, as though the *soil* of Great Britain made a slave free; but that is a legal fiction. Evidently, it is only when a slave (so called) comes *within the reach of an English court* that his freedom is declared. At that time the American colonies were beginning their quarrel with Great Britain, but had not renounced allegiance. All the colonies were subject to the common law of England;

and if in Virginia and Jamaica there had been a judge as upright and able as Lord Mansfield and a philanthropist as zealous as Granville Sharp, it would seem that slavery might have been dissolved by a few judicial trials.

This decision was of vast importance in opening the eyes of the British public to the essential illegality of a system morally so iniquitous. Honest, plain men were emboldened to look to the bottom of the case, when the shield and screen of law was removed. What if Parliament were to enact that in some county in England five persons out of six should become the property of the sixth, just as horses and cows are, and that the progeny for ever of these thus enslaved should be slaves ? Would it be within the competence of Parliament so to vote ? Or if by mere violence a part of the community were enslaved to another party, and Parliament and the courts were infamously to connive at it, would *custom* ever make the iniquity equitable, and vest in the violent oppressors a right of compensation when no longer allowed to defraud men of their dearest natural rights ? Every freeman who justified insurrection against royal tyranny was necessarily led to justify slave insurrection against their masters, however he might shudder at possible fierce retaliation for past injuries. Thus the mental revolution of England was begun, and in spite of the distraction of two dreadful wars—or we may say three—against the American colonists, against the French Republic, and, after the short peace of Amiens, against Napoleon I., the movement was at length carried to completion. But the interval between the decision concerning James Somerset and the Act of 1833 which emancipated the slaves, just exceeded half a century. This largely depended on the vicious implication of the English Ministry in the system.

Most of the colonies had independent local legislatures, and the apparent power of the British Ministry was limited to vetoing their Acts. Not but that they generally stood in such awe of insurrection that a force of British soldiers was needful to them, which force any Ministry could withdraw if they were contumacious. But they made sure that no Ministry would *dare* to expose them to possible massacre; insomuch that the Jamaica Legislature, in a pet, threatened to send the English soldiers home. In every practical sense the power of our Ministers was certainly limited in striving against the desperate mischief which the connivance of their predecessors had established. But there was one recently acquired colony in which the power of the crown was not restricted— Trinidad, a considerable island, ninety miles long, fifty broad, opposite the mouths of the Orinoco. It belonged first to the Spaniards, then to the French, and was captured by Abercrombie so late as 1797. Mr. Pitt was then in full power. A glorious opportunity was offered to this advocate of freedom to annihilate slavery in Trinidad; but apparently he had not the heart to carry out his own principles, even where he had no need to count votes. He was probably as afraid to encounter the ill-will of the West Indian planters, as Mr. Lincoln to meet the frown of Kentucky. Not only was this precious opportunity lost, but the Ministry were put afresh into the very evil position of themselves acknowledging, regulating, and establishing slavery in an island where neither the English Parliament nor any old routine hampered them. This false position they bequeathed as an evil legacy to their successors. Those who were themselves "regulating" a strictly illegal inhumanity in Trinidad and Guiana, could do nothing but seek to regulate and soften it in the other colonies. To declare for freedom was to condemn their predecessors, and some of themselves. Thus they were (so to say) constrained to justify slavery as such, to censure only any extremes of cruelty, and to maintain that the master had earned by the long custom of fraud and oppression a right to compensation (just as did Mr. Bruce, now Lord Aberdare, concerning the publicans —the renewal of their licences by negligent routine had given them a *moral right* to continued renewal!)—and these Ministers were to conduct the process by which alone freedom could be established. A most unpromising conjuncture!

To these difficulties of the position was added a religious controversy. It could not be pretended that either the Old or the New Testament forbade slavery as a national institution; it was a manifest fact that Paul exhorted slaves to obey their masters, "as service to Christ;" nay, that he sent back the fugitive slave Onesimus to his Christian master Philemon, and did not command the master to enfranchise the slave, nor to pay up the wages of which he had defrauded him, but contented himself with begging forgiveness for the slave if *he* had stolen anything, and merely urged to receive him as a brother in Christ, since Paul had converted him. Liberal interpreters may give excellent reasons why the conduct of the Apostle cannot be a law of life. But of course the slave-owners, both in the West Indies and on the American continent triumphantly claimed the great Apostle as on their side; and, what is remarkable, they carried with them in their advocacy of "the letter which killeth" (to use St. Paul's own words) not the ignorant vulgar, but the more educated and refined, who ought to have discerned the broad principles of justice and morality preached by the Apostle, to be paramount over isolated texts and detail of conduct. It cannot be doubted that sympathy with wealth and aristocracy was the cause: thus the more accomplished clergy of the Episcopal Churches became apologists or advocates of slavery, while the less educated Nonconformists stood up for freedom and right.

Yet each party claimed the Bible as on its side. In Jamaica, by far the largest of our West Indian islands, there was already a bishop, and it is only too clear that he drew his inspiration from the planters. What is more deplorable, our bishops in the House of Lords were never on the right side. In 1852, Sir George Stephen, writing a short retrospect, observes that reformers in England had one advantage over the American Union—namely, in titled leaders. "Royalty lent us countenance in the person of William, Duke of Gloucester; Lord Lansdowne, Lord Grenville, Lord Grey, and many peers of minor note gave their unqualified support." "The bishops— No! the less we say of their Right Reverend Lordships in connection with slavery the better." John Wesley had seen slavery in America, and called it *the sum of all villanies*. The Methodists, the Baptists, the Independents, and the Episcopal *Low* Church (to which Wilberforce belonged), and eminently the Quakers, were zealous for freedom, and chiefly from these *religious* circles the mass of our abolitionists came, despite of Onesimus. Zeal for missions arose chiefly from the same ranks. The High Church in the colonies desired to be on pleasant terms with the colonists, and succeeded; but the Nonconformist missionaries were always on very unpleasant terms with them. It could not be hidden from the planters that these missionaries pitied the sufferings of the slaves, and were trusted by them; out of which a belief arose that they fostered disaffection, and ran as close as they dared to stirring up resistance. In every insurrection the white men, through panic, became ferocious and uncontrolled. The home authorities never knew how to deal with an insurrection; for while they dared not justify it, their consciences did not condemn it, and they abhorred the indiscriminate cruelty of the planters or their agents. Two outrages against missionaries excited vehement indignation in England. The one was the destruction of a Methodist chapel in Barbadoes, as a part of the persecution of the missionaries. This was about 1825. The white population of all orders were guilty. The magistrates exulted in the outrage, some of them were said to have taken part in it. When Mr. (afterwards Sir Fowell) Buxton brought the matter before Parliament, Mr. Canning, as Ministerial leader in the Commons, reprobated the conduct of the whites most severely, and moved a vote of address to the Crown (which was unanimously adopted by the House) assuring his Majesty of their readiness to concur in every measure needed for securing ample protection and religious toleration in all his Majesty's dominions. Yet no white man was punished or censured, though in 1816, after an insurrection of the blacks, numbers of these had been massacred in cold blood.

The other outrage was in Demerara during the panic of an insurrection, October 1823, against the Rev. John Smith, a missionary from the Congregationalists (London Missionary Society). In time of actual peace he was tried, not by a jury, but by a court-martial at the drumhead, and condemned to death as having incited the slaves to an insurrection—an entirely false charge. They did not dare to execute their own sentence, but they threw him into a hot and pestilential prison,—treatment of which he died before free pardon from England was able to reach him. A burst of indignation had come from this country, Churchmen and Nonconformists uniting to demand justice; yet Mr. Brougham's motion in the Commons concerning it was voted down, as the Ministry would not break with the planting interest.

Yet in a circular from the Government, attributed to Mr. Canning, " mitigating measures " were recommended to the colonies, such as might prepare the negroes for freedom. Especially the discontinuance of flogging females was urged. The last proposal was discussed in each colony separately, and *voted down in every one.* Young lads were set to whip their own sisters. Mr. Charles Buxton* gives an extract from a Jamaica newspaper, to show how the planters of that island received these mild and very partial recommendations of the Home Government (*Jamaica Journal,* June 28, 1823): " We will pray the Imperial Parliament to amend their origin, which is bribery; to cleanse their consciences, which are corrupt; to throw off their disguise, which is hypocrisy; to break with their false allies, who are the saints; and finally, to banish from among them all the purchased rogues, who are three-fourths of their number." The excessive cruelty with which the whip was often used, could not be kept secret; but from the nature of the case, it was easy to reply that any facts attested were exceptional. In the Crown colonies an overseer was allowed at his own discretion to inflict twenty-five lashes (each lash generally drawing blood) on any negro, male or female; in the other colonies thirty-nine lashes were allowed. The evidence became worse and worse, the more it was inquired into; the papers laid before Parliament in 1824 were full of frightful details. Mr. Charles Buxton, in his excellent little book, observes that according to the sworn returns from the *four* Crown colonies, there were 68,921 floggings in the two years 1828-29; and according to general report, the full legal number of stripes was ordinarily inflicted. But what could not be explained away, was the awful fact of the dying off of the population. This is only to be expected where eighteen hours of work are exacted in the sugar harvest. However, in eleven islands, which also sent returns, the slaves decreased in twelve years from

---

* *Slavery and Freedom.* Longmans, 1860.

558,194 to 497,975. Everywhere, we now know, field labour thus destroys a slave population which is not recruited by a slave trade.

Meanwhile the popular movement was becoming irresistible. From 1772 onward, Granville Sharp had continued to exert himself, and in 1787, became chairman of a committee of twelve persons, the nucleus of the Anti-Slavery Society. *All but two were Quakers.* Sharp began the colony of Sierra Leone at his own expense, by sending thither a number of negroes whom he met in the streets of London. Till his death in 1813 he continued such philanthropic action. But the Society thus formed was soon strengthened by eminent and zealous coadjutors. The names of Clarkson and Wilberforce, Lushington, Denman, Mackintosh, Stephen, Zachary Macaulay (editor of the *Anti-Slavery Reporter*), Henry Brougham, live in honoured memory. Sir William Dolben began with the claim that the slave *trade* should be "regulated and conducted with humanity"! On approaching the problem practically it was soon found that nothing but total prohibition could succeed. So it is, when avarice and wealth have organised any huge scheme of mischief. The same thing was experienced in "regulating" slavery, simply because the masters were adverse. But here, for a little while, the Spanish colonies, it seems, held out to us [perhaps to President Lincoln] a false light.

These colonies had been formed under a monarchy practically absolute. The marvellous and execrable enormities of such men as Cortes and Pizarro had presented the Kings of Spain with Transatlantic dominions; but Charles V. rather shuddered at Cortes, and felt no gratitude for a valour which so little respected royalty. By his laws of the Indies he sincerely intended to protect both the native Americans, who had become his subjects, and the stronger African race, imported to fill their places. The royal power did effectually prevent the chronic slavery under Spain from ever being so bad as under freer States—England and Holland. One very important point alone shall here be noticed. To this day in Cuba, the nobler parent determines the rank of the offspring: the child of a freeman is free, though the mother be a slave. One might have thought that national pride would have claimed the same privilege for the children of an Englishman. But terrible to say, with us avarice overpowered both parental instinct and personal pride; our colonists decreed that in the case of mixed blood the children were all slaves. Thus the male profligacy, which tended to advance freedom in the Spanish colonies, tended in ours to multiply slavery in its most hateful and demoralizing form. A man's own children became his slaves—his *cattle*, and could be seized for his debts; his beautiful daughters might be sold as articles of voluptuousness. As an old overseer in Louisiana said to Mr. Olmsted, "There is not an estate here, but the grandchildren of a former proprietor are whipped on the field." But in the Spanish colonies, despite of plentiful cruelties where men were despots, the sentiment was far better than in ours, and there was no enmity against colour. Hence, as soon as they obtained liberation from Spain, the problem of emancipation was started by themselves, and solved differently in different colonies. One method was, to allow to the slave one day in the week as his own (in addition to any previous arrangement), and to fix a maximum for his price; then to enact, that when he could earn and pay a fifth part of his price, he should have a right to buy a second day free, leaving only four days in the week for his master. Thus an active and strong man bought first his own freedom, and afterwards that of his wife, and one helped another. In a climate where wants are few and the crops abundant, the slaves so rejoiced in the process of self-liberation, as not to brood over the injustice which withheld immediate unbought freedom. A second method was to declare all children born after a certain day to be free; or, indeed, both methods might be combined. The practical result was, that, in one way or other, all the Spanish colonies got rid of slavery. Mexico, which had an arduous struggle against Spain, and scarcely established a firm government until 1824, immediately proceeded to abolish caste and slavery, and effected the latter finally in 1829. Reports of the proceedings in the Spanish colonies, no doubt, reached the English Ministers, although neither by commerce nor by politics was there for a while any regular connection with them. Hence arose various schemes for gradual emancipation. The simplest and most plausible was to decree freedom for all children born after a certain day. This very measure was proposed by Lord Melville in the beginning of the century, but he did not succeed in carrying it, and apparently it was not renewed; yet it is evident that the Ministry from 1820 onward were bent upon some *gradual* form of emancipation, which should save the interests of the planters, and be in harmony with the principles and action of their predecessors. They did not understand, that when masters desire freedom for their slaves, many modes are open which will give mutual satisfaction; but that when the masters stubbornly resist, then only one method can succeed—total and immediate freedom, followed by regulations which make the freedmen socially, industrially, and politically independent of the master's resentment. The more the Ministers exerted themselves to "regulate" the slavery, the more bitter and violent did the planters or their substitutes become. Those who now say that the freedom ought to have been graduated, and that immediate emancipation was fanatical, simply show their total ignorance of the history—their folly and presumption.

Mr. Fowell Buxton had become in Parliament the avowed leader of the Abolitionists, when Mr. Wilberforce, through growing infirmities, withdrew from public life. On May 15, 1823, Mr. Buxton brought forward a motion that "slavery ought to be *gradually* abolished" (so little of obstinate fanaticism was there in the Abolitionists): but the Ministry was frightened at being pledged to anything, and put forward Mr. Canning (an eloquent speaker for freedom) to oppose Mr. Buxton. Yet his "amendment" was nearly to the same effect. The matter was to be left in the hands of the Ministry, but the House was to profess its anxiety for emancipation at the earliest moment compatible with the welfare of the slaves themselves (!) and the pecuniary interests of the planters. Mr. Canning plausibly stated, that "in the colonies the British Constitution *was not in full play.*" The Ministry, in fact, did not know how to enforce the ordinary rights of *free* negroes. But his liberal intentions were believed to be so sincere, that it was thought wiser by the Abolitionists to trust him, and hope for the best. No one had attributed to the Tory Ministries of this century any superiority of talent. Mr. Canning was their only brilliant man; but many of them were highly respectable and worthy in private life, and were sincerely shocked that human beings should be deprived of the most elementary rights, and have no security against fantastic cruelties. The most despotically inclined of them, Lord Castlereagh, was driven to self-destruction in 1822, by a creditable sensitiveness that his Continental policy had issued in nothing but mischief to Italy and Sicily, with the near prospect of the undoing of English work in Spain. The death of Lord Castlereagh (who had very recently become Marquis of Londonderry) was just in time to stop Mr. Canning from sailing to India as Governor-General, and installed him as Foreign Secretary. Though he could not save the constitution of Spain from the armies of France, while the Spanish King was treacherous, with Russia and Austria as allies in reserve, yet he sent a little army into Portugal, and told the combined sovereigns, in the hearing of Europe, that England by the stamp of her foot could raise up war against them in the heart of their own kingdoms. He likewise acknowledged the independence of the Spanish American colonies, all favourable to negro freedom, by which act (as he incautiously boasted) he "called into existence a New world to redress the balance of the Old." He also successfully instigated President Monroe to issue the celebrated declaration, that the American Union could not be unconcerned at any attempt of European Monarchy to establish itself on that side of the Atlantic. In short, this year 1823 was the first severance of England from the despotic Continental policy; it sent a throb of pride and confidence through the nation, and was a potent reinforcement of free sentiment in the ranks of the English gentry. Lord Sidmouth, Lord Bathurst, Sir George Murray, Mr. Huskisson, and of younger men Mr. Peel and Lord Palmerston, were all scandalised by the details which the Government received of West Indian cruelties, which not only went unpunished, but did not lower the credit and honour of the perpetrators.

To rehearse the dreadful accounts of intense cruelty and harassing miseries revealed to the Colonial Secretaries in official documents, would require many painful pages. Different colonies differed in degree of atrocity, yet everything seemed possible everywhere, and prevention or redress nowhere. Starvation and flogging were quite ordinary; but far more exquisite cruelties passed unreproved. The planters in the Bahamas, in reply to the

circular of his Majesty's Colonial Minister, passed Acts
to amend their slave laws and improve the condition of
the free coloured people; but when their new code
reached Lord Bathurst (1824), he pronounced the injustice of many of the enactments to be so manifest, that
he "assured himself" the Colonial Legislature would
remove them. But that Legislature replied by impugning
the English suggestions as injurious to them, and avowed
that "a strong sense of the great impolicy and absolute
danger of change compelled them to refuse to alter their
laws any farther."

In Barbadoes, Mr. Moe, Speaker of the Assembly, in
transmitting their new code to England, called it "a
splendid work, which would endear their remembrance
to posterity;" but Lord Bathurst was highly dissatisfied
with the new code. Yet Jamaica and Demerara, with
the Mauritius, seem on the whole to have been the worst
colonies. The missionary Smith well earned his murder
from the planters by his plain remonstrances against the
cruel treatment of slaves. "If it be asked," said he,
"are there not authorities to whom the injured slaves
can appeal for redress? Yes; but many of these are
owners of plantations, and perhaps allow their managers
to practise the same abuses. It would seem that some of
them consider it a greater crime in the negroes to complain of their wrongs, than in the master to inflict them.
The complainants are almost sure to be flogged, and fre-
quently before the complaint is investigated, unless indeed
listening to the master be called investigation. But even
where the justice of the complaint is undeniable, the
result is often such that the negroes cannot tell whether
the law is made to protect the oppressed or indemnify the
oppressor." No wonder that the planters did not like
missionaries! The Rev. Mr. Austin, of Demerara, a
respected clergyman, who was made a member of the

Court of Inquiry concerning the insurrection, attested
that the instructions given to the negroes by Mr. Smith
had eminently tended to prevent bloodshed; indeed, had
actually saved the lives of men who were now seeking
Mr. Smith's life. Yet, on the whole, the judgment of
Mr. Knibb, a Baptist missionary in Jamaica, seems to be
sound. He said that where a negro accepts the Gospel
spiritually, it softens and tranquillizes him; but the en-
lightening power to the intellect, which all teaching
gives, goes wider abroad than the spiritualizing power.
To learn something of the outer world, of its nations and
its powers; to reflect on themselves and their slavish
relation to one equally mortal, equally responsible to
God; to see and feel how different was the missionary's
behaviour to them from that of their master—had all an
electric effect, not contributing to the stability of slavery.
The planters of Demerara answered Lord Bathurst's circular defiantly: declared that their right in their slave
property was as complete as anyone's right to any property, and claimed to send deputies to England to argue
to this effect before the King in Council. Lord Bathurst
and his colleagues would probably have been satisfied if
they could have won for the slaves the most elementary
rights, such as, that a husband should have his own wife
sacred to him, that the honour of girls should be safe,
that the whip should not be used indiscriminately nor
cruelly, nor at all to females, that young children should
not be taken away from the mother, that the evidence of
slaves and black men should be heard in court, that all
judicial sentences should be strictly just, and no punishment excessive or peculiar, such as rubbing pepper into
the eyes and salt into wounds: but not one point could
be made sure. The planters were willing, for instance,
to concede to slaves a nominal marriage, but only with
the addition, "provided that it in no way prejudice the

owner's rights." Of course to make the wife an object inviolable to the owner's will, or to forbid his selling her away, *did* prejudice his fancied rights. Slaves were heard in court, but not only were not believed when they complained; they were far oftener punished for complaining: while if a pretext were wanted for punishing (perhaps hanging) a slave for an alleged scheme of insurrection, the evidence of a single slave was greedily accepted and acted upon. Thus the Ministers were checkmated in their schemes of *gradual, moderate, judicious* reform, and perhaps lamented too late that Lord Melville's scheme of freeing all children born after a near date had been opposed.

In the year 1828 a judicial sentence was pronounced that much afflicted Abolitionists. A negro woman of Antigua, called Grace, had visited England and returned to Antigua; and the question arose, whether after becoming free by touching English soil (such was the faulty way of putting the case) she could be seized as a slave in Antigua. It fell to Lord Stowell, a revered and venerable Judge in the Admiralty Court, to pronounce on this matter.* He was elder brother of the late Lord Chancellor Eldon, both of them intense haters of novelty, under whatever pretext of reform. If the advocate of the woman had alleged that the fact of English courts accounting her free proved that her original slavery *was an illegal piece of violence*, Lord Stowell might have been forced to another decision; but conveniently for him, that topic was not mooted. He argued in his award, that " Innumerable Acts of Parliament that regulate the condition of slaves *tend* to consider them as mere goods and chattels constituting part of the value of estates;" that " Colonial slavery has been *favoured* and supported

---

* It is called " his last decision." He retired from the bench in 1828, aged eighty-three.

by our own courts, *which have liberally imparted to it their protection and encouragement*" (an astonishing imputation on English Judges); he further said: "he trusts that he shall not depart from the modesty which belongs to his situation, and (he hopes) to his character, when he observes, that ancient custom is generally recognised as a just foundation of all law." When a judge of exemplary fairness in all international disputes shut his eyes to the main question, whether the violent detention of a woman in slavery, which was pronounced lawless in England, was not equally against English law in our colonies; when he further made custom and connivance a just basis for hideous iniquity, this sent a thrill of indignation into Abolitionists. In fact, Lord Stowell proceeded to call slavery a *crime !* "Emancipation," he said, "can only be effected at the joint expense of *both countries* (the colonies and England), for it is in a peculiar manner the CRIME *of this country.*" Marvellous judgment! Our population were in no complicity with it, but only certain planters of the West Indies, the Ministry, and (if we believe Lord Stowell) the *Judges*, who, he says, "liberally protected and encouraged it." Therefore he followed them in promoting "crime." However, the slave-owners were jubilant, and felt themselves in a legal sense much stronger than before. It became abundantly clear, that neither the Tory Ministers nor Tory Judges were willing to treat a purely moral question from its moral grounds. The same thing was soon to appear in a Whig Ministry.

In one important matter Tory Ministers had acted the Abolitionist with a high hand. In our American War of 1813-14, our Ministry invaded the American continent and *called the slaves to liberty.* They could not more emphatically disown the doctrine that slaves were private property; this was remembered by the English Abolitionists. The bold claims of the West Indian planters further opened the weakness of applying to *their* case schemes of gradual abolition such as had suited in some of the Spanish colonies. Men are not willing to have one-sixth part of their "property" taken away; of what use is it (asked the Abolitionists) to require the planters to give to the slaves one day in the week free, if they regard the slaves as their property? Again, as to the slaves buying themselves and their wives or children, may not the planter say he prefers to keep his property, and will not sell it at any price? It became more and more manifest that the nucleus of the whole controversy lay in the questions, " Can *innocent* men be justly made the chattels of other men? If a felon be ever so justly enslaved for life, would it be just on that account to make his children and children's children slaves? Can that be just concerning the children of men who are cruelly torn away from their native land, which would not be just concerning the children of felons? Can any long duration of such oppression confer a right of continued oppression? If there is to be compensation, is it not due from the oppressors to the oppressed?" No doubt, all these considerations were as clear as daylight to the earliest Abolitionists; but inasmuch as freedom could only be gained through the Parliament and the Ministry, they did not wish to run too far ahead of those who had to be convinced. When the Quakers and Nonconformists took up among the people the argument for freedom which Wilberforce and others pleaded in Parliament, the zeal of lecturers and speakers from the platform was ever on the increase. Scarcely any of these earnest men were paid for their services. Only at the last, in a few exceptional cases and for special reasons, was anyone paid; yet for many years no advance adequate to the necessity was made—apathy prevailed with the public. The reason at last appeared: no sufficiently *broad principle* was laid down. To force the planters to limit their stripes to twenty-five instead of thirty-nine, or to bring the slave to a magistrate to be flogged instead of by an overseer, public instinct felt, could bring no permanent result. At last the broad truth was promulgated (a Quaker lady is said to have originated it)—"Man by his moral nature never can become a chattel, therefore *to uphold slavery is a crime against God.*" "Until then" (testified Sir George Stephen) "we found the people apathetic and incredulous of our success, when the press, the Parliament, and the bishops were against us; but at last we had sounded the right note and touched a chord that never ceased to vibrate." This may be called fanaticism; but it is only by those who do not know what justice means, and are superficially acquainted with human nature.

Mr. Canning died, much lamented, after being for a few months Prime Minister, in 1827. In his short term of Premiership he achieved the Treaty of London, out of which sprang the deliverance of Greece (a little Greece, truly) from Turkish oppression. All England had sympathised deeply with the oppressed, and the voices of praise for brave insurrection had echoes reaching to the West Indies. An enfranchisement of Nonconformists in 1828, and of Catholics in 1829, followed. English newspapers were eagerly read in the West Indies, and the slaves became interested. In 1830, Charles X. of France, after conquering and keeping Algiers, because of an insult to his ambassador, violated his coronation oath, and was ejected from the throne by a popular rising.

The success of this French insurrection set all England agog; for we did not like to be behind the French in liberty. An insurrection of Belgium against the mild and equitable rule of the King of Holland followed, simply from the dislike of Catholics to a Protestant sovereign. Next came the uprising of Poland against the tyranny of the Archduke Constantine and against his brother the Emperor Nicolas: the Polish Constitution had been violently overthrown some thirteen years earlier by Alexander I. That by the way. The important thing was, that the slaves in many of the West Indian islands became greedy for the public news of Europe. Some one was generally found able to read out the newspaper to the rest. When they learned how vehemently brave insurgents were praised, a warm zeal for freedom was kindled in many hearts. Happily they read also that the people of England abhorred slavery, and were exerting themselves for their emancipation. The hope of obtaining freedom peaceably, restrained them from violent action. The Reverend John Barry, a Wesleyan missionary, who had resided twenty-seven years in Jamaica, attested that zeal for freedom had become an unquenchable passion there; and that when a number of them were executed after a recent insurrection, most of them died glorying in their fate, saying that if they had ten or twenty lives they would sacrifice all, sooner than return into slavery. The Duke of Wellington, in the close of 1830, seeing the storm of liberty upon him, resigned on a trivial pretext; Lord Grey came to the front, and at once pronounced for Parliamentary reform.

King William IV. and the Court yielded at first, but the House of Lords was obstinate, and a dangerous two years' struggle ensued. Meanwhile, matters grew worse, especially in Jamaica, which alone was equal to all the other West Indian colonies. In 1831 parochial meetings were openly held, in which the planters declared in violent words, that they would rather renounce allegiance to the British crown than allow the slaves to be freed. After this, they complained in a memorial that their slaves had been deceived into the belief that their freedom had been decreed in England, but withheld by their masters; and that this had led to insurrection. If it was true that this notion had been propagated among the slaves, evidently nothing so much propagated it as the conduct of the planters. But some insurrection there certainly was in 1832, which was speedily suppressed and cruelly punished. In Montego Bay alone, near a hundred slaves were hanged or shot, and one Baptist slave was flogged to death by five hundred lashes. Even magistrates assisted to pull down the chapels of the missionaries, as previously in Barbadoes. All these events could but embitter the negroes in other colonies, on the news reaching them. The Marquis of Sligo, a Jamaica proprietor, about this time, wrote thus to Sir Fowell Buxton: " When I went out to Jamaica, I thought that the stories of cruelty were merely the emanations of enthusiasts ; rather a caricature than a truth. But before I had been very long in Jamaica, I had reason to think that the reality has been far underrated. This, I feel convinced, is the fact." As soon as the new Ministry could gain free action for colonial affairs, it found the question of slavery in a truly critical state. According to a modern phrase, the relations were severely strained. Expectation among the slaves was intense. Any rude disappointment of hope might have caused insurrection, spreading as a flame from island to island. Public opinion in England would not endure the extinguishing of such a conflagration in blood, if the Whig Ministry could have lent themselves to it. The planters collectively might quickly lose, not their "property" only, but their lives ; as many as were not absentees. The Ministers saw themselves forced to act, and that quickly. The Abolitionists in that first Reform Parliament were numerous, but the Ministry had an enormous preponderance and could not be outvoted. The Colonial Minister, "Mr. Secretary

Stanley," afterwards Earl of Derby, was fluent of speech, ardent and flighty, vain, inexperienced, and utterly superficial; yet on him chiefly rested the conduct of this great measure. On reading his speeches at this distance of time, the weakness of the Government measure amazes one. In the preface to his first Bill, he avowed that "the only point to be discussed was, what is the *safest, speediest, happiest* way of effecting the final abolition of slavery; since the nation had now loudly and for a length of time declared, that the disgrace of slavery should not be suffered to remain part of our national system." He went on to recount, that after a unanimous vote of the House in 1823, certain "ameliorating measures" had been suggested to the colonists; but these had been "unheeded and disregarded by ALL the Colonial Legislatures." "Eight Bills were sent to them in 1826 by the Secretary of State, and not one colony would adopt a single Bill out of the whole eight; nay, they expressed lofty indignation at our interfering with what was their exclusive business." He proceeded to quote Mr. Burke on the inutility of trusting the Colonial Legislatures in the matter of the negro, because they will never *execute* the law. "The law does not carry with it *the executory principle*," in Mr. Burke's words. Who would expect, after this, that the speaker was about to give to the colonists the task of training the negroes for freedom in a seven years' apprenticeship? As an apprentice, the negro had no motive to work; for he was not to receive wages, and the whip was taken from the overseer. Sad experience had proved in Jamaica and elsewhere, that if a humane master, fresh from England, put a sharp limit on the stripes of the whip, the quantity of sugar enormously decreased. This apprenticeship was the height of stupidity, and could only aggravate difficulties. Popular opinion ascribed its origination to Henry Brougham, now become Lord Chancellor Brougham, a vastly different man from his former self: but the present writer knows no proof that that rumour was true. However, in this first Bill "Mr. Secretary Stanley" proposed a *loan* to the planters of *fifteen* millions, with a requirement that they shall sacrifice a *fourth part* of the labour of the slaves, who were to be allowed to buy their own three-fourths time, and were to be registered as apprenticed freemen. He volunteered to state his own opinion, that it would be quite unjust to expect the planters to repay the loan of fifteen millions; but the slaves ought to pay it, or a part of it: the rest might be borne by this country, unless indeed Parliament thought fit to convert the loan into a gift.

Viscount Howick (the present Earl Grey) vehemently protested against the continuance of the existing system for a single day, and insisted that, instead of the slaves paying anything to the masters, they ought rather "to receive compensation for past services and unrequited labours." Mr. Fowell Buxton also and others were highly dissatisfied with the proposals. This debate went on till May 14th, 1833.

Not to trouble the reader with further details, the *loan* of fifteen millions was finally changed into a *grant* of twenty millions, by two hundred and eighty-six ayes against seventy-seven noes; and the Ministry, against protest, insisted on calling it "compensation." Children under six years old were made free, so were all the negroes, nominally; then why compel them to labour for seven years unrequited? This forsooth was "the *safest, speediest, happiest* way" of liberating them!

We may well ask, How had the planters deserved this large gift or payment from our innocent nation? If the Executive Government winks at crime, does crime become rightful, and is the nation unable to forbid it without paying the criminals? Such was the doctrine of a majority of the Grey Ministry; certainly not the present Lord Grey, who always looks earnestly at the just and right. At any rate, the twenty millions bought up the worth of all the estates, and we might have claimed them as Crown property, and have given to the negroes independent freeholds; though of course no sugar would have been forthcoming for many years in that way. In the Mauritius notoriously the slave trade has been largely carried on even after 1807. But somewhat must now be said as to the worth of West Indian property at that time.

One word first on the laziness imputed to the negroes. They had twenty-six days in a year to work on their own allotments, and by this work they fed themselves— that is, by one day out of fourteen. Surely this denotes how well they worked, when they would themselves enjoy the fruit of their labour. A negress of Berbice complained bitterly that her mistress never gave her clothes, yet punished her by tearing her clothes in pieces; hence it would seem that the negroes often clothed themselves, as well as fed themselves. After the nominal freedom given in 1833, a negro might buy his own complete freedom : but no maximum price was fixed. He was valued by a stipendiary magistrate from England and two local justices; hence the ablest negro had to pay most. Even so, the Rev. Mr. Knibb attested that in Jamaica a full thousand negroes had in three years worked out their entire freedom, while only one-fourth of their time was their own. How fatuous is the complaint of idleness in "black Quashee!"

But now, as to the masters and overseers, were not *they* idle? After the slave trade came into full activity, they did not need to care how many slaves they killed by overwork; hence by force of the whip the estates

were for awhile highly productive. When George III.
came to the throne, was perhaps the very acmé of
flourishing sugar estates. But the culture was very
wasteful. Even the richest tropical lands will not bear
crops for ever with very partial manuring. The only
manure was carried in a sort of bowl on a slave's head.
The plough was not used; roads were hardly thought of;
the hands of unwilling men and women were the only
motive force. Meanwhile, the wealthiest of the planters
became absentees, and lived extravagantly in England;
many became Members of Parliament; some rose to the
peerage. The planters were manufacturers as well as
agriculturists. There was no economy on the estates
when the master's eye was removed, no reserving of
capital for better manufacture or less prosperous times.
The overseer, or manager, often kept more than one black
or brown mistress, and freely used the resources of the
estate for his own pleasures; nor were the managers
always honest in other ways. The mercantile agents
also made their harvest out of the estate; and if a loan
on mortgage were required, things soon went from bad
to worse. When the slave trade was forbidden, the fatal
blow was struck. Yet already in 1792 the Jamaica
House of Assembly reported that in the course of twenty-
two years one hundred and seventy-seven estates had
been sold for the payment of debts, and more than
eighty thousand executions had taken place, for a total
of more than twenty-two millions sterling. Bankruptcies
abounded up to 1807, through manifest recklessness.
The same ruin (Mr. Charles Buxton observes) came on
the Dutch colony of Surinam, where, out of nine hundred
and seventeen plantations, six hundred and thirty-six
were abandoned, though no philanthropists there teazed
the planters. In our West Indies the planters had a
monopoly of the British market; even sugar from

British India was highly taxed, as a bonus to West Indian sugar. This did not suffice. They obtained bounties on their sugar, as well as protecting duties. The latter were computed to mulct the people of England of at least one million and a half sterling, which in eighteen years (from 1815 to 1833) alone amounted to twenty-seven millions; and in 1833 the West Indian estates were worth very little. Already in 1830 Lord Chandos presented a petition from the West Indies setting forth "their extreme distress;" they earnestly solicited relief from Parliament; the distress was unparalleled; affluent families were reduced to penury; the *West India Reporter* said that without speedy relief numbers of planters must be ruined. They had killed off the negroes, had exhausted the soil, had lived extravagantly, and saved no capital, therefore could not pay wages; numbers were deeply mortgaged; they were liable to insurrections through the enmity which their wickedness had brought about; and after they had received much more than thirty millions in gratuities, bounties, and protecting duties, Whig Ministers insisted that they *deserved* "compensation," and settled it by the claims of the planters in London, whose goodwill (they fancied) would make things work smoothly in the colonies. Never was there so monstrous a price given for a property so rotten and already so laden with unjust gifts. But the Grey Ministry was overwhelmingly strong; and the anti-slavery party, dreading to lose the crisis, submitted; while they grudged the apprenticeship more than the twenty millions. The public were so delighted to secure the main point, that they forgot all beside.

Mr. Charles Buxton thinks it clear, from the debates in 1831 and 1832, that the real cause which brought round the Parliament collectively to the conviction that slavery could not continue and must be legislatively extinguished somehow, was the undeniable decay of the slave population. Without new importations of slaves all the islands must become worthless. This, and no considerations of humanity, nor regard to the public voice, was the overwhelming argument. That the terrible decrease in the number of the negroes was caused by overwork and cruelties, was rendered certain by the fact that the women were more numerous than the men; also afterwards, by the steady increase of the black population when freedom was gained.

The Whig Ministry took one step farther. They undertook, it is said, to give a promise, as a bonus to free sugar, that slave sugar (as of Brazil) should be excluded from our markets. How the promise of a Ministry can bind Parliament, is not clear; but both the anti-slavery party (in its narrowest sense) and the planters much reproached Lord John Russell and Lord Palmerston for breaking through this arrangement in 1846. These Ministers ascertained that no free sugar was sold on the Continent; for the cheaper sugar from Brazil drove it out. No discouragement whatever to slave sugar was brought about by our exclusiveness. The sole result was to offend the Brazilians, and almost ruin our trade with them. No doubt, Brazil and Cuba fancied they were going to have an extended trade, when their sugar was admitted to England. A temporary increase of the slave trade was an unhappy, unforeseen result, for which Lord Denman and others did not cease to reproach the Whig Ministers, though Sir Robert Peel supported them. The West Indian proprietors actually claimed both the promise given to them and the apprenticeship as "part of the compensation." Jamaica had a virtuous abhorrence of slave sugar, while she continued most tyrannical to the freed blacks. In all the islands the apprenticeship worked very ill, as every man of common sense ought to have foreseen. The Marquis of Sligo, Governor of Jamaica, condemned it, and at once set free all his slaves, advising others to do the same; but he had few imitators, except in Barbadoes. During the apprenticeship, when a negro desired to buy his own time of his master, he was charged in Jamaica *two shillings and sixpence* a day as its value. But as soon as freedom was complete, the planters who wanted labourers valued their work as worth only *one shilling* a day. From this and other frauds, besides the ill blood from old cruelties, many could not get field labourers at all. Moreover, the freed women no longer worked in the field. Nevertheless, on the few estates where good wages were paid punctually, no difficulty occurred.

It is needless here to pursue the miserable tale—how, after the apprenticeship was arbitrarily terminated in Parliament (not least through its exposure by the devoted efforts of Joseph Sturge and other good Quakers), the Colonial Legislatures hankered after a new slave trade, under the name of apprenticed coolies, and taxed the negroes to import them. Jamaica, as usual, had the pre-eminence in tyrannical legislation and unjust application of public money; until their Legislature itself became unendurable to Tories as well as Whigs. Space does not permit to detail the deeds of Governor Eyre. Suffice it to say in outline, that in 1865 an alarming outbreak of some hundreds of coloured men took place; that martial law was proclaimed in a limited district; that Governor Eyre arrested a coloured member of the Legislature, his political opponent, Mr. G. W. Gordon, the advocate of justice for the blacks; carried him by force into the district where civil law was suspended, had him tried under martial law by two young officers, and hanged. Many besides were hanged; men and women were flogged with piano-wire, houses of black men were burnt, and after all semblance of insurgency or resistance was put down, violent horrors continued. The Assembly passed a Bill, justifying all Governor Eyre's proceedings, which interposed insuperable difficulties to prosecuting him. The English judges were aghast at such lawlessness and at the frightful precedent. Neither a Whig nor a Tory Ministry could for a moment defend it; and though Governor Eyre was not punished, nor Mrs. Gordon (the widow) compensated for losses, the verdict of England was pronounced against the whites of Jamaica. They were summoned to resign their legislature, and did not dare to refuse. An English Governor was sent out (Mr. John Peter Grant, of Indian celebrity) to rule them despotically, and from that day the condition of Jamaica has slowly improved. The chief thing needed has been to take power out of the hands of those who in former days were accustomed to be tyrants.

If space allowed us to pursue the argument, it would most abundantly be proved that every approach to a modified slavery, such as disguises itself in apprenticeship of coolies, is always as mischievous as unjust; and that the vigilance exercised by the Aborigines Protection Society is never superfluous. But the pen must be checked. In future articles the yet greater question of Slavery under the American Union will be treated.

APPENDIX.

In India under the Hon. East India Company slavery was found to exist, unknown to the English nation. How it was dealt with, I have learnt only by private talk with an old servant of the Company.

Official orders were sent by the highest authority to

every one acting as judge, that every Court in India should disown the cognizance of Slavery as a legal system. Thus, if a slave escaped and the master or mistress claimed him, the English judge refused to lend aid in restoring him, but pronounced him free, and warned the public that they must behave to him as one free.

In this way they took no notice of slavery, so long as the slave from habit and from decently good treatment acquiesced in his lot; but only when his case came into court. Hereby they believed that the institution would wear out, and indeed be mollified by fear of escapes. Also, they avoided the great evil of slaves suddenly freed having no home, no resources and no custom of trade. So diverse is the stage of civilization in different parts of India, and so small a fraction of residents in India of the English-born, that in many an unvisited corner there may still be some *domestic* slavery, especially under polygamists.

PART II.

NEGRO SLAVERY IN THE AMERICAN UNION.

From "FRAZER's MAGAZINE," February, 1879.

In a previous article on Negro Slavery in England, it has been stated how gladly Virginia received her first cargo of slaves—only twenty in number—from a Dutch ship, in the year 1620. From that time the importation went on rapidly. Some twenty years later, slaves were introduced into New England; in each case without legal enactment or authority. Nevertheless, when in 1646 a cargo was brought to Puritanical Boston, a cry was raised against the sellers as malefactors and murderers. The magistracy committed the guilty men to prison, denounced "the heinous crime of man-stealing," in short, ordered the negroes to be sent home at the public expense. In that early stage the national conscience was not yet blinded by custom, and frankly applied the doctrine, that the receiver (or buyer) is as bad as the thief. In May 1701, Boston, in Massachusetts, instructed her representatives "to put a period to negroes being slaves," and American writers say they were thwarted by the mother-country, that is, probably by the English governor. But no vigorous measures were taken against the actual slavery nor against the demoralizing doctrine which with it oozed in from the southern colonies, until that great commotion, the War of Independence. At this era, the history of North America sharply separates itself from the history of England.

In the year 1776, when the war was getting hotter and hotter, the celebrated Declaration of Independence was issued, by the consent of Northern and Southern statesmen, on July 4, and was signed by every member of Congress. In the second paragraph it avowed: "We hold these truths to be self-evident: that *all men are created equal:* that they are endowed by the Creator with certain *inalienable* rights: that among these are life, *liberty*, and the pursuit of happiness: that to secure these *rights*, Governments are instituted among men, deriving their just powers *from the consent of the governed*," &c. After many such generalities, it proceeded to recount "the injuries and usurpations" of which "the present King of Great Britain" (George III.) had been guilty; at length "appealing to the Supreme Judge of the World for the rectitude of their intentions," the signatories avowed themselves absolved from all allegiance to the British Crown; and with a firm reliance on Divine Providence, mutually pledged their lives, their fortunes, and their sacred honour for the support of this declaration.

"The injuries and usurpations" which King George III. had inflicted on the colonists were mere trifles in comparison with the frightful wrongs perpetrated by the colonists on the innocent African population. Of all the Congress-men who signed that document, not one slave-master was so brazen-faced as to deny that African negroes were *men*. It was reserved for the hardened impudence of the nineteenth century to invent as "philosophy" the doctrine that negroes are not men, and have not the rights of men; and that while the States abounded with mulattoes and quadroons, whose colour faded through the brown and the yellow into the white, the profligate and proud "Caucasians" had produced such progeny, not out of women, but out of female beasts. Such was the doctrine by which, twenty and thirty years ago, cultivated writers of the South shamelessly tried to evade the pinch of the broad declaration : "All *men* are created equal, and liberty is their inalienable right." Negroes, said these polished gentlemen, are *not* men. No approach to such impudence was possible while the colonists were fighting for their "natural rights" against English royalty. The worst that English tyranny could or would have inflicted was political subjection; every slaveholder's conscience told him how small an injury that was, in comparison to a slavery which treated men and women as cattle. The South did not then attempt to justify slavery, but apologised for it as an heirloom to be regretted, a burden that could not *at once* be shaken off. Since in the North there were few slaves, and those chiefly in domestic service, philanthropy had a less arduous contest. Even before the peace with England, which was not until 1782, Massachusetts established for herself a new constitution in 1780. In the next year a Bill was found in Worcester County against a white man for assaulting a black whom he called his slave. When the white man appealed to the Supreme Court of Massachusetts, he obtained a reply based on the decision that the *Declaration of Independence* forbade slavery; a decision which for ever settled the question in Massachusetts. Although this celebrated document was not embodied into the after constitution of 1789, which embraced *all* the States in a more intimate union, the Northern lawyers were able to insist, that in every doubtful point the Constitution must be interpreted in harmony with that Declaration, on which the independent existence of the States was founded.

But when peace came, the position of all the States was critical and anxious. Unless they were firmly knit into a single body, they were liable to civil war, and to be variously embroiled by European intrigue. Large debt had been incurred in their struggle. Some fixed sources of revenue must be attained, and some steady central authority, before they could have security for their future. Weakness might entail anarchy. Without union and harmony they would meet with no respect from Europe; hence mutual concession appeared to be their first wisdom, and the leaders persuaded themselves it was their first duty. Only two out of the five Slave States stood up as champions of slavery, South Carolina and Georgia. In the former, the cultivation, first of rice, next of indigo, had proved highly lucrative ; and it is noted that the planters who took the lead in resisting freedom were descendants of the Huguenots, who a hundred years before had fled from the cruel bigotry of French misrule. Georgia had a still more infamous record. Established under George II. (1732) with a charter expressly forbidding slavery, because of the great mischiefs, social, moral, and economic, *already experienced* in Virginia ; nevertheless a fraction of the State, corrupted by the contagion of South Carolina, did not cease to agitate, drawing the clergy to its side by aid of Scripture texts, until by petitions to England they obtained a new charter permitting slavery. Of this cruel and pernicious concession George III. was held guilty; for assuredly no minister could have wrung from him consent against his will or judgment. Georgia thenceforth was peculiarly virulent towards the Indian tribes as well as to the Africans.

Virginia was, on the contrary, philanthropic; North Carolina well inclined. Both States had done their part honestly, by forbidding the African slave trade (in 1776 and 1774) so far as their own citizens were concerned. Unhappily the Virginian philanthropists, like the vast majority of statesmen, thought it unstatesmanlike and perhaps fanatical to make *justice* paramount in public action. Patrick Henry, Mason and Randolph, Washington and Jefferson, all saw the evils, the iniquities, the horrors of slavery. Because the institution was *so* evil, *so* unnatural, *so self*-destroying, they thought it was not needful for *them* to destroy it. Like President Lincoln, they treated the vital rights of Africans as a card with which a politician might play at his own discretion. Like him also, they were blind to the wisdom of the precept, "Strike while the iron is hot," so necessary in a revolution, when new principles are to be introduced. Washington talked, but did not act. He could not exhort and denounce while he kept his own slaves. He was satisfied to be a dilettante speculator in future history by prophesying that slavery could not stand. By his will he liberated his slaves *after his wife's death;* but the lady, more sensitive of conscience, liberated them at once. His great eminence, his immense authority, not merely in the crisis of victory, but precisely in the years when action would have been most fruitful, forces us to accuse him as the one man who probably might have overthrown slavery, yet from personal interest did not make a single effort. The decisive reply of milder Southerners in this century, when pressed in argument against slavery, habitually was: "Surely if in Washington to hold slaves was not villany, it cannot be much harm in me." It is vain to plead that Washington feared to alienate the two restive States. He had the conscience of every energetic and worthy man on his side. He could appeal to the signature of the Declaration of Independence by the delegates of those two States. His vehement action and exhortation would to a certainty have carried his own State (which possessed half the slaves in the Union), and must have given an immense impulse to freedom. If, after trial, he failed to make freedom the law of the Federation; if the rest shrank from excluding the two States from the

Union, yet these would have been admitted under far severer conditions, and perhaps with a year of complete freedom pre-stipulated. By liberating his slaves after his wife's death, Washington made it clear that for no reason but his private convenience had he detained them at all in a condition which he avowed in talk to be unjust and odious. In striking contrast to all this was the conduct of Thomas Jefferson, to whom neither his countrymen nor our writers appear to have awarded sufficient honour. Jefferson evidently had far more intense feelings as to the pestilential nature of the evil, and lost not a moment in acting against it. As early as 1774, when the war was only beginning, he avowed in a convention in Virginia that the abolition of slavery was the first thing to be desired; but that to make it valid a prior step was needed: the introducing of new slaves must be stopped, "a project in which unhappily *his Majesty's veto* had hitherto defeated their attempts." His energy was well-timed and successful. In 1781 he wrote his celebrated *Notes on Virginia*, which for some reason did not appear until 1784, printed in Paris. He writes as a true-hearted man, whose soul and conscience are affected. He entitles the slaves "*citizens*" and "*our brothers.*" He describes the depraving effect of slavery on white children—evidently writing from personal observation— and avows that *in case of a slave insurrection God has no attribute which can take sides with the white man.* In his own State he further attempted to carry a law establishing freedom after a certain date, but he failed. The present writer cannot learn that Washington gave him the slightest aid or countenance in this very mild and urgently needed remedy. In 1784 Jefferson proposed in Congress that slavery should be excluded from all the territory ceded to the Union by Virginia. His Bill was lost by the accidental absence of one delegate, and next year when introduced again was out-voted. After this, it would seem, he despaired of legislation, and looked with sad presentiment to chastising events as alone compulsory: hence in his later career he was passive, though to his dying day deploring the evil, which had grown stronger and stronger.

Rice and indigo were old products in South Carolina, but at the Revolution cotton was new. No one then conjectured how great was to be the importance of that crop. In a very few years after independence was attained, the growth of cotton increased prodigiously. It is related that in 1783, just after the peace, eight bales of cotton were seized by the Custom House at Liverpool through unbelief that they really came from America; but in 1789 the cotton crop (chiefly from South Carolina and Georgia) reached to a million pounds, and in 1801 to nearly fifty millions. This was the article which chiefly, when zeal for freedom had become more languid and anxiety for a stronger Union keener, in 1789, made a peaceable legislative abolition of slavery finally hopeless. The founders of that Constitution were resolute not to admit into it the word slavery, nor for some time from any quarter was the doctrine heard that the Federal Government had no power over the institution of slavery; indeed the delegates from Georgia and South Carolina in vain clamoured for a clause which would disown such power. But while slavery existed within the limits of the Union, it was impossible to avoid some mention of the thing, however distasteful the name. If they would not abolish it, some compromise was inevitable, and it arose in three branches: the first concerning the African slave trade, the second concerning the taxation for the slaves, the third to provide for the case of fugitives. Some may count as a fourth the Ordinance of 1787, which forbade Slavery between the Ohio and the Mississippi. For it may be argued: "To forbid it over one area was to sanction it elsewhere." Yet if W. Lloyd Garrison himself had had a vote concerning that ordinance it is difficult to believe that he would have failed vehemently to support it, on the ground that to narrow the area of slavery was an achievement much to be rejoiced in.

The compromise concerning the African slave trade was briefly this. No legislation against it was to be made before 1808. South Carolina had compunctions and struggles, but from 1804 to 1808 imported largely. When that year was reached, Congress became competent to forbid it, and did forbid it. It would seem that, before the date just named, a new interest had arisen, hostile to the African trade, in the internal slave trade of the Union itself. Virginia especially, which was accounted the Paradise of the Union by reason of its soil and climate, was so wasted by the reckless improvidence of mis-culture, that its chief gains began to accrue from breeding slaves for the market. North Carolina was in much the same case. Of course, the price of these slaves was likely to be enhanced if the supply from abroad was stopped. This argument can hardly have failed to add sensible weight to the humane movement against the infamous cruelty of slave hunts and the horrors of the middle passage. The African trade was in 1808 not only forbidden, but was pronounced to be piracy; a most just sentence, to the height of which English legislation did not advance. But it is not likely that the slaveholders of Louisiana and Georgia ever ceased to murmur under the loss of the African supply; and as years rolled on, the intense cruelties of the inter-State slave trade furnished them with ample arguments. Macaulay, in the House of Commons, denounced its wickedness as more atrocious than that of the African trade. Perhaps rhetorical impulse here carried him too far; but such an utterance from a man so accurately informed, to an audience so intolerant of enthusiastic exaggeration, is notable enough. Indeed, there was always some smuggling in of slaves from Africa or Cuba; and their comparative cheapness so inflamed avarice and stimulated indignation in the States which had to buy from within the Union, that a Southern society at length arose for the re-opening of the African slave trade, a result which would undoubtedly have followed if the South could have established her independence in the late American civil war. In 1857 Governor Adams, of South Carolina, in his address to the Legislature, formally denounced the prohibition of supply from Africa as "a violation of the Constitution." As an illustration of the temper and tone of Georgia, the reader may be interested in an extract from the speech of Mr. Gaulden, a Georgian delegate to the Charleston Convention in 1860, just before the rebellion broke out. He spoke as follows:

I am a Southern States'-Rights man. I am an African slave-trader. I believe that slavery is right, morally, religiously, socially, and politically; and has done more good for this country and for civilization than all other interests put together. . . . I would beg my friends of the South to come up in a proper spirit. Ask our Northern friends to give us our rights, and take off the ruthless restrictions which cut off the supply of slaves from foreign lands. As a matter of right and justice to the South, I would claim of the democracy of the North to grant us this thing: and I believe they have the patriotism and honesty to do it, because it is right in itself. I tell you, fellow-Democrats, that the African slave-trader is the true Union man. The slave-trading of Virginia is more immoral, more un-Christian in every point of view, than the African slave-trade. We are told upon high authority that there is a class of men who strain out a gnat and swallow a camel. Virginia, which authorizes the buying of Christian men, separating them from their wives and children, from all the relations and associations amid which they have lived for years, rolls up her eyes in holy horror when I would go to Africa, buy a savage, and introduce him to the blessings of civilization and Christianity. It has been my fortune to pay from 1,000 to 2,000 dollars a head, when I could go to Africa and buy better negroes for 50 dollars apiece. I represent the African slave-trade interests of the State of Georgia. I am proud of my position. I believe that the African slave-trader is a true missionary and Christian, &c.

He proceeds to declare that if the right of buying from Africa is not granted, "the glorious Union shall be disrupted, and go out in blood and night for ever." Undoubtedly the wicked cruelty of the inter-State slave trade went a great way towards lessening the advantage gained for humanity by the compromise, which at length prohibited slaves from abroad.

The second compromise concerned direct taxation. Were slaves, like cattle, to be accounted the property of the owner, and his tax to be proportioned to them? If taxation was by the head, were slaves to be taxed and the masters or the local State made to pay? No principle could be found as a basis if the slaves were not citizens, were not foreigners, and were not cattle. A compromise therefore was inevitable. *Five* slaves were to be counted, both in taxation and in voting, as *three* freemen. This gave to the South an advantage in voting power, and to the North an apparent advantage in the increased taxation of the South. But a very few years deprived the North of the bonus, such as it was: for the Federal Government was supplied by the custom houses, and in part by sales of the public lands. Direct taxation fell into disuse. The voting power gained by the South was almost immediately turned to account, and not only strengthened the slave power, but inflamed its ambition and its audacity. The too confident belief that slavery was dying, and would soon vanish, damped resistance to this compromise, yet a few spirited men vehemently opposed. Governor Morris, of Pennsylvania, declared it to be a premium on atrocious villany. If a buccaneer from Georgia or South Carolina tears away Africans from their homes, and "damns them to the most cruel bondage," he is to be rewarded by a vast increase of his voting power. If he carried off fifty unhappy victims he would have thirty-one times the voting power in the Federal Government which the innocent and honourable citizen of Pennsylvania possessed. That was indeed a startling result; but its abolition is *at this moment* complained of in the North as having made bad worse. The three-fifths rule is abandoned; the negroes have the vote nominally, but in various States of the South the armed clubs of violent and reckless white men intimidate the negroes from voting, while the collective State uses the entire negro vote, five negroes now counting for five citizens. The poison of slavery is not as yet at all worked off. If a president be now elected in the interests of reaction, it will be by the white men of the South quelling and yet using the negro vote.

The third compromise concerned fugitive slaves. In the original draught of the clause they were called persons held in *servitude ;* but on the motion of Mr. Randolph, of Virginia, the phrase was altered to "held to *service,*" so anxious were even the Virginians not to stain the Constitution with slavery. Service belongs to freemen, servitude to slaves. Apprentices are "held to service." There was nothing in the mere phrase to justify anyone in saying that the Constitution had recognised slavery. But in order to enforce this clause of the Constitution a special law was needed, viz., what is called the first Fugitive Slave Law of 1793. It is marvellous with what speed the slave power assumed predominance, no doubt because the citizens of the free States were busied with industry and domestic concerns, the great mass of them thinking little of politics; while the slave-owners everywhere disdained labour, were supported by the toil of others, and turned their leisure entirely to the art and science of living on plunder. We in England heard so much of the Fugitive Slave Law of 1850, that we are apt to undervalue the former law. The difference to the slaves and to the free blacks was little or nothing; to the free white man it was great. Both laws enact that any man from the South may enter a free State, arrest at pleasure anyone on its soil, carry him before a magistrate, claim him as a fugitive slave, and if by oral testimony or affidavit he can persuade the magistrate that his claim is just, then the person arrested *shall have no appeal to a jury*, with a view to establish that he is *not* a fugitive, but a legal freeman, possibly a citizen and native of the State. Very few white persons were likely to be dragged into slavery by the want of jury defence; but to free blacks it was certainly a real danger. No doubt, in consenting to the law, the North believed that a magistrate would be a valid protection. It was scarcely till forty years later, when the South had become proud of slavery and had filled the high Federal offices, including the Supreme Court, with its audacious supporters, that the North felt the humiliation imposed by this enactment. But the new law, on which the haughty infatuation of the South insisted, punished every freeman in the North if he would not actively aid the slave-catchers.

From the era of the first Fugitive Slave Law is dated the steady advance of slavery as a doctrine and as a power. The ministers of Christian Churches became its warm advocates *on Scripture grounds* first in Georgia, before the War of Independence; the same influence rapidly spread in every direction. Commerce becoming energetic in the new Union, quickly gave to numbers of Northerners a pecuniary stake in the Southern funds. Presidents elected in the interests of slavery kept the poor whites of the South firm on the side of the aristocratic slaveholders, by dangling before them the hope of petty Government appointments. Patronage, on the same condition only, was given to Northern ambitious aspirants; but actual Southern men had a most disproportionate share of the embassies and secretaryships. In the slave States neither the press nor public meetings nor open speech was free, though the duty of the President was to uphold such freedom. Thus the landless whites of the South were kept in political ignorance. Suddenly, and quite unforeseen, a great event occurred. Napoleon the First, aware that he could not save the French colony of New Orleans from the English fleet, sold it in 1802 to the American Union in order to prevent the aggrandize-ment of England. To possess the mouth of the Mississippi, and hereby its entire course, was a first-rate advantage which no American statesman could possibly reject. It opened to them at once visions of greatness before un-dreamed of. Instead of being a country on the borders of the Atlantic, hemmed in, it might be said, by the Alleghany Mountains, they embraced the entire valley of the Mississippi, with no civilized power to limit their westward extent. A glorified future rose up to their imagination. Nothing seemed able to limit their rising grandeur but civil war among themselves.

In the outset there were only thirteen States, of which only five retained slavery, and only two of these were bent upon retaining it permanently. But Virginia, Mary-land, and North Carolina had largely exhausted their soil by tobacco, and had more and more become breeding States. To have a new market in new slave States for the sale of their human cattle was to them a great bonus. Besides, according to the rules of the Constitution, every State had two representatives in the Senate or Upper House, a House which has two important powers above those of the Lower House of Congress. By keeping a majority in the Upper House, the slave power would always be able to veto legislation which it disliked.

Hence all those in the interest of slavery were eager for new slave States. Jefferson avowed it to be most doubtful whether Congress had the power so to tamper with the original Constitution; but the magnitude of territory overpowered all scruples. And in fact Tennessee had been separated from North Carolina in 1790, and soon after was admitted into the Union : Kentucky also was admitted early. Louisiana was the first new slave State admitted; but a long series followed. Florida was partly conquered from the Indians, partly bought from the Spaniards. When the North saw Louisiana, Missouri, Arkansas, Mississippi, Alabama, Florida admitted as slave States, they might well be alarmed; but a still graver affair arose in the matter of Texas.

The Spanish colonies, when freed from the yoke of Spain, soon took measures for terminating slavery. Mexico, on attaining comparative tranquillity in 1824, at once turned her attention to this object, and in 1829 effected it. Thus the Southern States of the Union found that in Texas, a Mexican possession, they had freedom close to their frontier. They had already made war upon Florida, and spent millions of public money to recover a few fugitive slaves. The same policy made them act the buccaneer against Texas, primarily in order to re-establish slavery. Ultimately they stole this large province from Mexico, first acknowledged its independence, next brought it into the Union, to the bitter resentment of the free States. President Polk presently made a war against Mexico by his personal act, against Constitutional rule, which gives to the Senate an entire command over war and treaties. A vast region was conquered from Mexico. California was expected to become a slave State : the same result was fought for in Kansas. One compromise after another was broken through. A new Fugitive Slave Law was imposed. In short, the North seemed (to a superficial view) helpless to resist; since her statesmen, through personal ambition, one after another failed to be staunch to freedom. The arrogance and audacity of Southerners, their high-handed dealing with citizens from the North, their lawlessness and ferocity, were intolerable and alarming. Yet the North meanwhile had grown in real strength prodigiously more than the South. Her citizens multiplied rapidly; nearly all new emigrants from Europe came to swell the numbers and wealth of the free States. Her middle classes were eminently industrious and inventive, while those of the South were mostly worthless vagabonds. In Pennsylvania were iron mines and iron works: great and noble shipyards abounded. The great State of Ohio had been added to the Union in 1801, a good balance against Louisiana. Then Indiana, Illinois, and the great North-West were a grand development of freedom. Maine and Vermont were also carved out of the original New England. The South was wasting from within by the various follies of slave culture and the reckless idleness of the "mean whites." When the crisis of civil war was approaching, the census showed that the hay crop of the North was alone equal in value to the collective crops of the South. The ignorance of the "mean whites" was on a par with their idleness and poverty. In 1838 Governor Campbell of Virginia informed his Legislature that more than one-fifth of the applicants for marriage licences could not write their names. On a far greater scale, on a much larger area, than in the West Indian Islands, slavery was proved to be ruinous to the soil, depraving to the masters, and weakening to the community, as well as cruel and degrading to its innocent victims. California and Kansas declared on the side of freedom, and the gain to the slave-holder from the new Fugitive Slave Law was contemptible. The Southerners were irritated, perhaps panic-stricken, by their own miscarriages, but only blustered and stormed so much the more; while their most educated men and their more polished clergy glorified slavery as a religious and sacred institution.

When the English Parliament in 1833 decreed freedom in all our colonies, the American slave-holders saw that an immense influence on the side of freedom would follow among all who talk English, if they did as their fathers had done—merely apologized for slavery. Indeed they had already disused that tone: but at this new crisis they more than ever assumed the tone of glorifying the institution, and presently attempted to found a philosophic justification of it from ancient history. In 1835 Governor Macduffie addressed the Legislature of South Carolina as follows:

No human institution is more manifestly consistent with the will of God than domestic slavery: none more conducive to the happiness of the African race. Instead of being a political evil, it is the *corner stone* of our republican edifice. [Alexander Stephens, twenty-six years later, borrowed this phrase, and sanctified it from a Hebrew Psalm.] No patriot will tolerate the idea of emancipation, at any period, however remote, or on any conditions of pecuniary advantage, however favourable.

Similar doctrine was preached from the pulpit. Unhappily the broad fact is undeniable, that shortly after the abolition of slavery by England the American Churches, North and South, more and more threw themselves on to the opposite side. It is notorious that in very numerous cases the chapel funds rested on slave property, so that pecuniary interest largely co-operated with a slavish devotion to the letter of Scripture as decisive of morality without consideration of circumstances. The press of the North most largely sided with the South. The prevalent sentiment of the commercial classes in the North was an extreme fear of losing business. The politicians dreaded lest the turbulent South, which talked at one time seriously of "Nullification," at another wildly of civil war, should really bring about this result. Northern States had also a physical aversion to the negroes which was not shared by the South; they had neither black nurses nor brown concubines. As Mr. Seward coarsely expressed it in England: "We hate slavery; but we hate the negroes still more." Great numbers who abhorred slavery, yet shrank from advising that the blood of Northern whites, who had extirpated the evil at home, should be shed to extirpate it elsewhere; hence, while hating the institution, they deprecated any downright and frank utterance against it which would irritate the South. Anyone guilty of this misdemeanour was tabooed in society, was shunned in the market, was perhaps glanced at from the pulpit, and often persecuted by threats and warnings in anonymous letters. It was a real time of terrorism to the few courageous speakers for freedom.

The "Martyr Age" of the United States has been generously and vividly depicted by Harriet Martineau. The times needed an enthusiasm which should be plain and free as that of prophets; brave as that of soldiers calmly risking life and limb; pertinacious and untiring; firm to withstand the frowns and authority of public men, the pretensions of religious teachers, and the bitter insults of fools who fancy themselves wise. If in such a time of struggle the much-needed enthusiasts had a dash of the fanatic, who can wonder? who can censure? The wonder is that so much meek gentleness and heavenly charity reigned in those involved in such a battle. The first honours must undoubtedly be awarded to W. LLOYD GARRISON and the brave, noble-hearted few who gathered round him, largely Quakers and women. The Quakers from early years were eminent in the cause of freedom, and have earned (an old Roman might say) immortal praise by their heroic conduct. To set free their own slaves, if the laws of the State permitted, or pay them wages and treat them as free, if no other way lay open, to assist fugitive slaves from slavery at their own great risk, appear to have been their uniform practice. But the encroachments of the slave power by working upon the compromises of the Constitution drove into them a hatred of the Constitution itself, to which the Garrisonians refused to take the oath of allegiance. Garrison denounced the Union as "a Covenant with Death and Hell," his favourite expression it would seem. The Bristol anti-slavery tract named above, which warmly sympathized with the Garrisonians, defined in 1846 their new political doctrine as follows:

"None of us *will vote* for any candidate for political office; because we should virtually pledge ourselves to the principles:

"1. Of delivering up fugitive slaves.

"2. Of quelling by military forces a slave insurrection.

"3. Of protecting slave States from foreign invasion.

"4. Of allowing to slave owners the three-fifth vote."

To carry their doctrine out, they invented a new pledge with the motto, *No union with slaveholders;* a formula which included the withdrawing from all churches with which slaveholders were joined. By this section a "disunion pledge" was circulated, which ran thus: "We, the undersigned, to clear our skirts from innocent blood, pledge ourselves to strive for the peaceable *dissolution of the Union*, as the most consistent, feasible, and efficient means of abolishing slavery." Garrison's own organ, *The Liberator*, discussed also various topics unconnected with slavery, concerning which the sympathizing Bristol tract mildly remarks, that perhaps abolitionism would be more benefited by their omission. To most of our readers it will be obvious at once, that if the Garrisonian doctrine of Quaker-like non-resistance and clain of disunion could have prevailed over one-half of the population of the North, the South would at once have been entire mistress of the position. In the end, *insurrection of the slaves*, which this section of the abolitionists pointed to, as the thing which would bring freedom if the Union were dissolved, would be anything but a way of peace. Of necessity the promulgation of such aspirations and such political exhortations gravely offended not only the Northern advocates of slavery, but thousands of its opponents. The South had indeed previously offered a reward for kidnapping or killing Garrison. Elijah Lovejoy, a noble and blameless enthusiast of freedom, met his death by a number of Southern bullets. An abolitionist seemed to the South as wicked and detestable a monster as a heretic to the mediæval clergy.

It would be an entire mistake to suppose that the Garrisonians had any scheme for liberating the slaves. They neither had, nor tried to get, any political agency for the purpose. Their sole function was, to arouse men's consciences by bold utterances of hatred and contempt for the vile injustice and cruelty inherent in the slave system; and herein they undoubtedly had great success, especially after they were reinforced by the eloquence of WENDELL PHILLIPS, a young barrister of excellent position, who despised the loss of friends and of worldly honour, and encountered all deadly chances in the cause of justice. Yet if the history be impartially considered, no practical results at all desirable would have come from the Garrisonian movement had not a much needed supplement to it arisen in another quarter; that is, in a political section called the FREE SOIL party. With this the celebrated Fremont of South Carolina was connected. Its doctrine was simply: "No more area shall be added to slavery;" for they saw, and the Southerners confessed, that the slave power must waste, unless aggrandized by new States. The wonderful victory of Kansas in a most unequal struggle animated them. Indignation was awakened in the entire North by the new Fugitive Slave Law, which taught the bitter lesson that they were all made slave-catchers by Act of Congress. The party called Whigs having become feeble, a new party with the name *Republican* arose from the Free Soilers to oppose the South and its Northern allies, who were called *Democrats*. The German immigrants, from hatred of Royalty, had generally joined themselves with the Democratic party; but after better understanding American politics, the mass of them came over to the new Republican party, which presently found in CHARLES SUMNER its learned, accomplished, elegant, and laborious leader. It is believed that to him is due the Republican formula, "Slavery is sectional: Freedom is national." He showed in many practical arguments that the Constitution which Garrison reviled as a Covenant with Death and Hell was based on freedom, must be interpreted by the Declaration of Independence, had been perverted and wronged by the lawyers whom Southern Presidents had promoted, and that it contained abundant weapons for fighting against slavery. Then arose the demand of suppressing the slave market and slavery in the small Federal territory called Columbia, which contains the city of Washington and the halls of the Federal Government; also a like demand of making every Federal fortress free soil, besides the non-extension of slavery to new States or territories. The freedom voted by the new State of California greatly encouraged the rising Republican party. They put forward Fremont as their candidate for the Presidency, not indeed expecting to succeed in the elections of 1856, but calculating on a large minority in that year, and on success in 1860. In both they were right. The Southern leaders freely avowed that to lose the Presidency was to lose their cause; that if a President were elected on the side of freedom, he would so distribute his patronage as to draw off the mean whites; he might insist on a free press and free speech in the South, and the slaveholders would be outvoted in their own States by the poor white men whom they despised and kept in ignorance. Besides, in the hilly regions, in what is now called Western Virginia, in the Blue Mountains and the Alleghanies, in Eastern Tennessee and the hill country of Georgia, there was little or no slave culture; the white men were comparatively industrious and honest, and by a small impulse were likely to take sides with freedom. Besides which, the Southerners were possessed with a fear that under a President elected by the North the Congress would stop the inter-State slave trade; a prohibition which was undoubtedly constitutional, if only the leaders of freedom would have consented to call the slaves *property*. The Southerners called them "property" everywhere else; but in the migration from State to State they called the slaves their *households*, and so had a right of passage with which Congress could not interfere. Yet they did not expect Congress under a President from the North to endure such evasion. They were agonized at the growth of the Republicans, at the wealth, population, and energy of the free States, which left them far behind in the race for all national greatness. Their apparent successes had brought them no real strength. Unless they could hold the Presidency firm, slavery would not stand for twenty years. Even so early as the year of Fremont's rejection for the Presidency, there was plenty of talk in the South about secession, *if* a President from the North were elected next time; but this talk did not come from the highest quarters in the South; —leaders were too prudent to be frank so early; by which the North was deceived, believing such utterances to be wild bluster and nonsense.

In fact, this course of events brought about just the most desirable result, of which the Garrisonians had no foresight whatever. If a part of the North—say, all New England—had renounced the Union as "a Covenant with Death and Hell," nothing would more have rejoiced the South. It was indeed the very scheme of the Southern leaders, if they had been successful, to *eject* New England from the Union: "to leave it out in the cold" was their current phrase. They hated and dreaded its doctrines of justice, its humanity, its energy, and its intelligence, all of which they called fanaticism. Had New England voluntarily renounced the Union, the fanaticism of the South would have been victorious, certainly for fifty, perhaps for one hundred years. All the States whose rivers flow southward, together with New York, would have fallen at once into the clutches of the slave power; and the future of the coloured race would have been more gloomy than ever. The friends of freedom in the South would have been betrayed. The African slave-trade would have been renewed, and slavery introduced into all the territories suited for slave culture. Illinois, Indiana, perhaps Pennsylvania, would have become Slave States. But when the South took its fatal plunge into disunion, its pro-slavery allies of the North were indignant and alienated. They had helped the South because they were dazzled by the vision of a Republic that should dominate the breadth of the continent. They had heard from the South no end of invective against the wicked abolitionists, who wished to break up the great Union, and lo! the South itself had done this very thing. Even Kentucky and Maryland declined to risk their fortunes with this Southern enterprize. All Americans knew that the whole valley of the Mississippi was and must be under a single power; that any attempt to divide it must lead to perpetual border war, and that the power which held the mouth of the great river was sure to become mistress of the whole. Every citizen of the North felt himself wronged and robbed by the attempt of the South to carry off the vast regions which had been bought chiefly by Northern blood and Northern money; regions in which each had a guaranteed right to travel and to settle. The South believed that the North would not fight, that all the slave States would secede in mass, or that if the North did fight, the South would get help from England and France. These delusions made one State after another imitate the headlong folly of South Carolina. The result justified the wisdom of Charles Sumner, and finally destroyed the slave power.

Before that end arrived, the South understood well that *Sumner*, and *not Garrison*, was their formidable enemy. For ten or fifteen years they were frantic against Garrison, but from the time that they understood his avowed zeal for disunion, their personal anger against his section seems to have abated. The leaders perhaps discovered that to preach disunion was to play their game; but their fury turned now against Sumner, and a man was found to perpetrate just what their enmity desired. While Sumner was sitting at a desk, writing in the Senate House, the ever infamous Preston Brooks, coming behind him unseen, struck him from his chair by a blow on his head from a cudgel, and while he lay on the floor, continued beating him on the head until he was insensible. Several senators stood by, but not one interfered to stop the ruffian. Charles Sumner was carried to his house more dead than alive. It was uncertain whether he would live, or, if he recovered, whether he would not be a helpless idiot. The ladies of the South contributed small sums in large numbers to buy a gold cane for Senator Preston Brooks, as a thank-offering to him for having vindicated the honour of the South. But how had Sumner insulted the South? By a speech in which he alledged by *argument* that a Slave-System was not (as the South boasted) Noble and Rightful, but essentially Barbarous, further, he demonstrated from *history* that in the War of Independence the South had not contributed troops for the battle-field in any proportion to the free North; dread of slave insurrection, among other causes, having crippled them. It was not known that a single newspaper of the South disowned the outrage of Preston Brooks; it was notorious that numbers of them warmly extolled it.

Upon this deadly attack Emerson observed: " It is the first blow of civil war." But it was in 1856. The rising generation of Englishmen need to learn the tyrannical fierceness, the atrocious perversion of morals, the mean wickedness, which slavery generates in the slave-masters, besides its unspeakable cruelties to the slaves, and its ruin to national strength and greatness, equally as to art and science.

PART III.

FINAL ISSUE UNDER PRESIDENT LINCOLN.

[Planned as a third Article in " Frazer's Magazine," but withdrawn.
It is since variously filled out.]

THE preceding has detailed how the Southern States of the American Union, goaded by pride, ambition and alarm, worked themselves into the *resolve* of breaking away from the North. That the reader may the better understand their temperament, a few more details may be added of events which preceded the final struggle under President Lincoln. South Carolina will give us one typical anecdote.

In this State the ratio of slaves to white men was greatest, and what Massachusetts was to Freedom, such also was South Carolina to Slavery. Georgia may have equalled her in insolent ferocity, but Georgia had fewer relations with the world outside. Its commerce did not compete with that of Charleston, the capital of South Carolina. To this emporium came ships from the Northern States, ships also from the English West Indies. Each was liable to have free negroes among their sailors. Free negroes in the South were rare, except in Louisiana, where the French left them ; and the very sight of a free negro was odious to men who did not at all reject black concubines. Foreign sailors in port are always glad of an outing, as a relief from the smells of a ship and its sad monotony ; but coloured foreigners were an ill-omened sight in Charleston, perhaps in the white man's imagination were an incitement of insurrection. Every wrong (say our lawyers) has its remedy : the South Carolinians had their own simple process. They did not wait for a dark man to land, but boarded the ship, took every coloured man out of it and lodged them in jail. A Charleston jail might not be over healthy, but it was not given them freely. They were kept there, as long as their ship remained in harbour; then they were charged for bed and board, and those who could not pay, were sold into slavery! Such at least was the complaint from Massachusetts. The authorities there sought redress through the President. The President could only use influence at Charleston. Redress to the commonwealth of Massachusetts consisted in fair words; the wrongs against their free and equal coloured men, sometimes reaching enslavement, continued: so they resolved to send an embassy of their own to Charleston, and selected as their ambassador Judge Hoar, a man much esteemed, of mild and urbane presence. From his gentle and just expostulations they hoped some result. He went, accompanied by his daughter only. And what followed? Simply this; that though Judge Hoar brought formal papers from the Governor and State of Massachusetts, the authorities of Charleston would not meet him, but a body of Lynchers with much rude insult forcibly carried back the Judge and his daughter beyond the limits of South Carolina. No redress to Massachusetts was given or pretended. That Palmerston and Russell tamely bore like ill-usage of their West Indians, cannot be asserted; simply because we have no evidence that they ever knew the facts. As in widely other matters, so here, their subordinates may have purposely withheld from public documents whatever the chief Ministers could not wish to proclaim that they knew. But their ignorance is likely to have been "official" only. How Rangoon was treated by us in 1852 because excessive port dues were exacted of two English ships, is a contrast curious and painful.

It was not South Carolina alone that ran mad with religious fanaticism. Some Northern Abolitionist ingeniously suggested that the South ought to raise a statue of ONESIMUS in every town, and thus diffuse the celebrity of him, who, in obedience to the apostle Paul, returned into slavery. In a still more exalted aspiration, the Rev. Dr. Palmer, of New Orleans, pressed on the South that its mission from on high was "to preserve and transmit to posterity its system of slavery, by obtaining for it the right to go and take root *wherever* Nature and Providence can support it.

(a.) From 1849 to 1858 various attempts were made to invade and possess Cuba by armed expeditions from the Southern coast, in secret understanding with malcontents on the island. But all these efforts failed, sometimes by the interference of the American Government, sometimes by the action of the Spanish authorities.

(a.) In furtherance of the same design a Conference was held at Ostend in 1854 between three of the United States' Ministers accredited to European Courts. These men,—Mr. Buchanan, of Pennsylvania, Mr. Mason, of Virginia, and Mr. Soulé, of Louisiana, — prepared a manifesto, which was made public. [It appeared in *The Times* with comments.] In this they had the monstrous effrontery to declare: "It is perfectly clear to every reflecting man, that, by its geographical position, Cuba naturally belongs to the United States. If Spain refuses to *sell* the island, then by all laws human and divine we shall have the right to snatch it from her." The Convention of the "Democratic" party, assembled at Cincinnati in 1856, virtually ratified this "Ostend Manifesto" by choosing Mr. Buchanan, one of its authors, as the candidate of that party for the Presidency.

(a.) In 1858, Mr. Buchanan, elected President, proposed to Congress to carry out the Ostend programme.

Mr. Slidell endeavoured to induce the Senate to allow the President thirty million dollars for the purpose of opening negotiations for the purchase of Cuba. At the same time Mr. Mason proposed, that discretionary powers, —including the employment of the naval and land forces of the United States,—should be conferred upon the President, to facilitate this coveted acquisition; but the *Senate* rejected both these propositions.

(a.) In 1854 occurred the marauding expedition of Walker against Nicaragua. His object was, not only to re-establish slavery in that country, where it had been abolished, but also to gain a base of operations against Cuba. His first purpose was temporarily accomplished: slavery was established by a Constitution prepared at New Orleans: but Walker and his party were soon driven out of the country.

In the elections of 1860 the Slave Power had hesitated chiefly between two candidates, Douglas and Breckenridge, which is believed to have damaged them; but a far worse cause even ruined them. A decision in the "Dred Scott" case by a judge in the Supreme Court was thus worded: "No coloured person has any right which a white man is bound to respect." Likewise the brave and noble death of "John Brown" had aroused a glow of enthusiasm in the North. John Brown had become a colonist of Kansas to save the territory from slavery; had there fought against the marauding whites from Missouri, and earned an exalted enthusiasm when victory there crowned the little army of freedom. He formed the grand idea of imitating these marauders by in turn invading a Slave State,—*not* to attack the whites, but to march the slaves

---

To secure accuracy of details, the paragraphs *(a)* are extracted from Dr. F. W. Sargent (second edition, p. 62, London, Hamilton, Adams & Co., 1864). In the Civil War, Mason reappeared as the Confederate Commissioner to England, Sliddell to France.

away. He crossed into Virginia with thirty-two men at Harper's Ferry, where the Shenandoah falls into the Potómac, and called on the slaves to take refuge with him. Virginia shivered with alarm from end to end, and soon gathered an irresistible force against him. He was seized and hanged; but his gentleness, his love of children, and the simple bravery of his death, deeply touched the Virginians, and with the North elevated him to glorious martyrdom.

The Northern Convention doubted between two candidates for the Presidency, Seward and Lincoln. Of these, Lincoln was regarded as the less advanced and less formidable to the South; indeed he had married a Southern wife. According to the logic current in those pre-elections, the candidate least sharply pledged has made fewest enemies, *therefore* has the better chance of success (since Hate is more active than Love), *therefore* more deserves support. The South confessed Lincoln's majority to be unprecedented. Allowance must be made for Lincoln's weakness, when we learn that in part he was selected for his leanings to the South. The Republican Party which he was supposed to represent, had two cardinal principles:

I. Slavery is only sectional; not Federal or National.

II. The Slave-Area shall not be further enlarged.

The conduct of Mr. Lincoln signally disowned the former. If he previously avowed his own principles, the deceptiveness of these " caucuses " would be put in a still stronger light.

In the months which intervened from his election to his stepping into office, his predecessor Buchannan and the whole outgoing party had made their oaths of office empty words. They carried off the money of the Treasury which was but the beginning of practical treason.

In December, 1860, the State of South Carolina (always forward with Georgia in zeal for slavery), issued a Manifesto to all the other Slave States, representing their common danger, if a man opposed to slavery became their President, and exhorted them to secede with her from the Union and thereby "to form a great Slave-holding Confederacy larger than all Europe." The answer was given in twenty-two days by the seizure of thirteen Federal fortresses with great Navy yards and arsenals and all their Ships of war. This was easy; for the treasonable connivance of President Buchannan had withdrawn all the garrisons. Meanwhile all the Northern Forts and Arsenals were emptied of arms and ammunition and the ships were sent southward or were in distant seas. The other States did not all at once put forth Manifestoes of secession, but their adhesion at heart could not be doubted. Every local leader who had aided in seizing the fortresses had broken his official oath to the Union.

But one voice highly honored in the South dissuaded secession, both as morally void of right and as more likely to fail. This was from Alexander Stephens of Georgia, a genuine devotee of slave-holding; who was for awhile clearsighted. He declared that the North had always given to the South more than its due in every political sense; that secession must unite the North in common effort, with the probable result that War would wrench every slave from their grasp.—His enthusiastic fellow slave-holders could not accept his gloomy forebodings; yet in rejecting his policy, showed their high estimate of him by electing him Vice-President of their Confederacy under Jefferson Davis as President.

It did not need in a middle-class Englishman any high education or rare access to books or travel over America, to be as wise at that moment as was Alexander Stephens. The North could not submit, without yielding the mouth of her great river, and ultimately its whole valley.

Notoriously to sanction the principle of secession was simply ruin of her grand future : still, we in England could not then know, how far the entanglement of Northern interest in slave property and the old political attachments under so many Presidents from the South, might bias all foresight. But *if* the North bravely insisted on punishing the rebellion, her final victory seemed certain ; for, the Free North was a complete nation without paupers or " proletarians." Its area was cultivated almost wholely by landowners, who were staunch for the Rights and Grandeur of the Union. The mass of its workers, in town or country, were the best educated in the world, the most accustomed to various machinery, and apt at new inventions of peace or of war. In numbers they greatly surpassed the freemen of the South, even if in these we count the hill-cultivators of the latter, whose hearts were chiefly with freedom. In the South was hardly a middle class ; the " mean whites " were poor, because Labour was despised : the North had abundance, because Labour was honored and highly intelligent. Such was the contrast. *But the rebels had counted on aid from without.* Liverpool friends of the South had taught them, that European Royalty would infallibly desire their success, and how much more they might hope from the English upper classes and from Louis Napoleon.

When March 4th, in 1861, drew near, and Mr. Lincoln was about to travel to Washington, information reached him of a conspiracy lying in wait, to kill him or carry him southward. The scheme, if real, was folly ; for a more decisive man, his Vice-President, would at once have stepped into his place. He altered his course and arrived safely ; but when inaugurated, barely knew how to summon a hundred trusty guards. The rebels easily raised and armed fifty thousand men of the " mean whites," accustomed to the field and to fire-arms. Our ambassador at Washington cannot have failed to impart all details to Downing Street.

A glorious opportunity was offered to our Cabinet, which it threw away :—*of course*, we may (alas!) say. All Europe honored England as the foe of slavery, not knowing that the justice of our nation never animated its rulers. If these had flamed out in wrath at the *breach of official oaths*, so deadly a danger to every Imperial Power, it would have seemed to all the Princes natural and reasonable. The English nation would have rejoiced, only a few caitiffs in the Commons House might have murmured, if in the name of the Government the Chancellor of the Exchequer had asked leave to offer to Mr. Lincoln the loan of fifty ships of war with all their accoutrements and stores, besides cannons and rifles and soldiers' kits as much as he pleased, so as to give him time to replace all that had been wickedly carried off by official treason. Such a manifestation of English sentiment would have appalled the stoutest of the rebels, and might have quelled the awful war before actual battle had begun. It would have made the Confederate Loan impossible. We should, without any sacrifice, have earned warm and priceless gratitude from all American lovers of freedom ; and could further, at cheap cost, have stipulated for Mercy to the rebels on their accepting an early termination of slavery. Fine imagination all this ! when perhaps the South had already taken close measure of Palmerston and all his crew, and sagely inferred, that he had no heart for generosity or justice.

What on the contrary did our Government do ? They sent a Mr. Massey to speak at Salford a speech intensely hostile to the North, ignoring the treason of the South and its purpose to diffuse and perpetuate slavery over the whole breadth of America, also the zeal of nearly all (except Virginia, *the breeding State*) to re-open the African slave-trade. He aimed, and utterly failed, to stir our working men into hostility with the North. They well knew the danger of *Cotton Famine* and that to them it might mean *Bread Famine ;* but they scorned to stave it off (if indeed that had been possible) by accepting complicity with slave-holders. On the contrary, in hope of crushing a just and industrious Republic, our Ministers were eager for the success of execrable buccaneers. So great was the moral dissent between Rulers and Ruled.—From Mr. Massey's mission, alike North and South learned what conduct was to be expected from corporate England. It soon was announced by Earl Russell that *" the North was fighting for Empire "* (really for its own solid continuous land and running streams), *"the South for Independence"* (really for discriminated freedom of rape and robbery). A heartless pack yelped to the chorus, that *" The success of the North being impossible, its acceptance of the war is blood-guiltiness. "* The Peers' House rose higher yet: when one of them triumphantly exclaimed : "The BUBBLE at last is burst," and the House joyfully accepted its meaning, that the Great REPUBLIC is irrecoverably destroyed.

"Magistracy will display the man, " was the motto of the Greek sage Bias. Foreigners seldom know how an American is likely to act. Of Mr. Lincoln we knew little more than that he represented the side of Freedom. His first business was to gain time and postpone battle. He ingeniously limited his own task. What he had received in trust as President, he was bound to keep, and to fight for it, if it were invaded; but what had been already seized, he had never received, and was not responsible for it. Therefore he could peaceably negotiate with the seceders. But when the demand to allow of "extending the area " of slavery was made, and he necessarily refused, it was discerned that he wished to gain time; so conference was broken off. But at the first moment of his power, while he was wholly unguarded, before the Free States had been able to show him their enthusiasm, some might think Fear unmanned him; but his fixed idea was, to win the rebels back by concession. Whatever its aim, his very first step was a prodigious blunder, and by its haste quite inexcusable. Ambassadors and Envoys to Europe ordinarily change with a new President. He might at least have given time for his own minister Mr. F. C. Adams to reach England and discuss matters with Earl Russell, a hereditary friend of freedom *(at least so reputed)* who then was our Foreign Secretary. Mr. Adams was a very cautious statesman; at home called "a non-committal-man," who might well have announced, that the President "earnestly desired peace, deprecated force as the means of reunion, and would do his best *not* to have to constrain the South." But before Mr. Adams could arrive, the President's circular to the old ministers in Europe had reached them, disavowing his *right* to constrain the South! It was (no doubt with great glee) instantly presented, and eagerly received in France and England. Then with "indecent haste" we proclaimed *the belligerence* of the Southern Confederacy, and *the purpose of England to be neutral* in their war. The effect of this edict was (1) to allow Englishmen to build ships of war for the South, which else would have been piracy: (2) to give value to Confederate bonds in the English market.

The question of Belligerence could only arise on the open sea, on which the South had shown not a single ship; England, forsooth, was *neutral* where she was not implicated. To Hungary, even when victorious over Austria, she refused recognition of belligerence, which would have enabled Hungary to buy arms from Turkey for defence against Russian invasion : now we gratuitously recognize buccaneers, before they are visible as a State. Mr. F. C. Adams complained privately, that on landing (at Liverpool I think) he was mortified to see Earl Russell's proclamation, to his own great amazement. Charles Sumner also was indignant at it. Neither permitted himself to blame Mr. Lincoln, whom (long afterwards) we sadly learned to have gratuitously smoothed the way of our Government to its evil course, and (we may say) almost suggested it. But the Hon. John Jay, in an elaborate memoir on the war, delivered at Paris in 1867 and published by our Anti-Slavery Society, justly lays the blame of this grave mischief on Mr. Lincoln himself. His Cabinet can scarcely have been formed. Our loyal citizens (says Mr. Jay) saw through the error and " step by step compelled the Government to relinquish its *temporizing, vacillating,* and *timid* policy." Whether these epithets are the worst that may be used of Lincoln's whole career, the reader will judge.

In the war of Hannibal a beaten Roman general quotes a celebrated sentiment from Hesiod, that he who has not wisdom from himself and will not accept it when propounded by another, is a worthless man. This formula tells pointedly against Mr. Lincoln. Working his way up without advantages of early education, he did not analyze the right and wrong of the American Constitution side by side with the rights of human beings, as did Charles Sumner; but when Sumner clearly set forth what each President owed to every slave, and did *not* owe to rebel States, Mr. Lincoln might have learned most profitably, yet uniformly refused. Sumner never could have been frightened by the strength of the rebels, because (be his straits what they might) he distinctly knew his own duties. Lincoln also *wished* to do his duty, but (so confused was he between seemingly contending claims) *his notion* of it had no fixedness. Sumner was in his own body a martyr of freedom under the brutal Southerners; yet whatever the cruelties of the South, he vehemently forbad retaliation of barbarity. He held the balance of Justice so firmly, that he was thought to be haughty. How can a mathematician pretend modest deference to one who fights against demonstration? How can a moralist avoid to be decisive and incisive, when sacred truth is garbled? Sumner was certainly disliked by many and perhaps was feared by Lincoln; who from first to last did the best things wrongly, though Sumner urged to do them at a right time and in a right way.

The Vice-President of the South, Alexander Stephens, became convinced that Lincoln was too timid to fight, and that the secession was already victorious. He thereupon put forth another oration, widely different in tone from the former. The North celebrated it as his "corner-stone" speech. In it he said: "We are now the paramount power of this Continent. The Halls of Montezuma lie open to us." (That is, we may conquer all Mexico and re-establish slavery there, when we please.) "Slavery is the stone which our first builders rejected, but now it is become the Head of the Corner. This is the Lord's doing, and it is marvellous in our eyes."

But, glorying in their strength, the rebel Confederacy forced Lincoln into war, by attacking and capturing Fort Sumter, on April 12th, 1861. Lincoln aimed to put them in the wrong, even in the judgment of men who made light of official oaths, but yet had some conscience against aggression by bloodshed. He now was able to say: "I did not *begin* the war: *they forced* it on me." He immediately called for seventy-five thousand men and elicited enthusiastic response.

Charles Sumner as Senator from Massachusetts laid a Bill before the Senate, propounding that the Federal

Power must observe Moral Law, International Law and Federal Law, but owed *no* duty to the *local* enactments of a State which had rebelled; therefore the Federal Generals should acknowledge no other distinction of persons on a rebel area, than that of loyal and disloyal citizens.—This was a mere deduction from a cardinal principle of the Republican Party.—Slavery is sectional, not Federal. Yet, apparently through fear of embarrassing the President, the Senate merely "tabled" the Bill, but took no further step.   To table a bill *reserves* it, does not *reject* it.

A foreign writer cannot accurately give explanation of votes, but we know that through the long possession of the White House by Presidents from the South there was in the North itself a very strong party who looked mildly on Slavery.   Whatever the latitude, there were many to argue, "Washington was a slaveholder: the system cannot be so very bad."   Though the Northern party called Democratic had largely rallied against the South in defence of the Union, yet in both Houses of Congress there remained numbers who did not wish Slavery to be then touched.   This may suffice to explain the apathy of the Senate, and ought never to be forgotten as an apology for the President for desiring the Slave question to remain temporarily quite in the back ground.

Invasion on the part of the North began from Missouri, where Fremont of South Carolina was made military commander on August 31st, 1861.   He was highly popular with his troops; and boldly proclaimed that he disallowed Slavery on the rebel area.   By necessary inference he accepted as free all slaves who fled to his camp.   His quickness to go ahead alarmed the President, especially since Fremont was said to *violate* (?) a superfluous Act of Congress which, on August 6th previous, had declared all slaves free who had been used in hostile service against the U.S.   Fremont refused to modify his proclamation when the President condemned it on September 11th. He forthwith resigned his command, apparently because he would not obey the cruel and stupid order to send back the slaves for their masters to punish. Thus unhappily this most celebrated Southerner, who was an enthusiast for freedom in his native State, a man gallant and splendid, honoured for his American travels, and eminent by his candidature of 1856, suddenly vanishes from this history. Instead of him Maclellan rises into prominence as a sustainer of slavery, and becomes Mr. Lincoln's favorite general. An ill omen of the war.

The Abolitionists (not Garrison) commented, that "Mr. Lincoln desired greatly to have God Almighty on his side, but was resolved to have Kentucky with him." Yet when Lincoln made his call for troops, Kentucky distinctly refused, and next month, as if to mend the matter, proclaimed "her own neutrality." Hereby she declared herself already in secession and *legitimately separate*. In that early stage Lincoln wisely refrained from driving these foes into hostility : but their State is directly accessible on three sides to Northern armies ; so that next year Lincoln was well able to call them severely to account, and had no excuse for petting them. But Kentucky was his native State.

He can hardly have been *ignorant* that in the second war against England (1813-14), slaves in New Orleans were forcibly enrolled by the Federal Government ; and for those slain in battle, repayment to their masters was refused, though the then President was on the side of slavery. *If horses had been seized, payment would have been made.* Thus the slaves were not accounted as cattle, nor as property, by Federal routine, but as persons, under duty to the Federal Authority ; as "citizens without suffrage." Whoever owes duty, especially dutiful exposure of his life for a sovereign power, obviously has a claim of protection from that power.—Mr. Lincoln never could learn this simple and certain morality, though the status of even slaves in relation to the Federal Government was written clear in the conduct of President Monroe.

The moral force of the Abolitionists became strangely divided. Wendell Phillips had supposed Cotton and the Dollar to be almighty with the North, but from the moment that Northern enthusiasm burst out, Wendell Phillips went over thoroughly to Sumner, and Garrison seemed to lose half his following. No doubt such was Mr. Lincoln's self-sufficiency, that in no case could the united influence of the Abolitionists Proper have moved him. Possibly Garrison's apathy was not prompted by trust in Lincoln, so much as by a sense of helplessness.

A solution of the immediate question, "Ought fugitives to be sent back to punishment?" was truly needful : for no fugitive any longer dared to approach the Northern camps; the generals had no local guides, and could not learn where the Confederates were in strength. Mr. Lincoln's *second great blunder* brought swift punishment on his brave armies, who were driven back with serious loss and permanent damage. But aid came from a quarter unexpected. Benjamin Butler, a lawyer of Boston, had been a vehement friend of the South from a belief that the Abolitionists were bent on breaking up the glorious Union ; naturally, when the South did this very thing, he joined the Republican party, as a loyal Unionist. His argument was substantially as follows. The President holds the slaves to be rebel property : well, so are horses. But if horses strayed to our camp, we should not anxiously send them back; nay, we should gladly keep them, because in war they may be used either *by* or *against* us. They are evidently *contraband of war ;* so therefore are slaves, even if the President rightly calls them property.—The public applauded, and we hear no more of fugitives being driven away.—Lincoln's minister in England, a very moderate Abolitionist, explained to the present writer how vehement and inveterate had been the refusal of the North to acknowledge the slaves to be *property* ; though hereby damaging their own legal right to stop the wicked Inter-State slave trade. And lo ! a President elected against slavery struggles against his own party to uphold the slaver's immoral claim !

Early in this war the bravery and success of the Germans in Missouri was eminent. This State, west of the Mississippi was quickly consolidated as outer bulwark of the North, and its first permanent gain.

The zeal of the North increased with the strain put upon it and with the increase of the Southern armies ; its chief early advantage was on the sea, because of its machinery and its skilled workmen. The Northern ships, constructed in hot haste, soon blockaded all the entrances along two-thousand miles of coast. In February 1862 the North had recovered six out of thirteen Fortresses originally seized. But alas ! The narrative must return to the aid which *England* gave to the South. In 1856 at the Congress of Paris after the Crimean war, Lord Clarendon proposed, in the cause of humanity, to forbid privateering. The Powers there present renounced it in their own names, and undertook to endeavour to obtain a renunciation of it from all other marine Powers. The smaller States agreed, but not the great American Union. Mr. Marcy, in the name of the President, said, that in a possible war, they had no war-fleet to defend their merchants, and unless England would renounce the assailing of merchant ships *even* in war, they could not sacrifice their right of commissioning privateers for defence. Earl Russell, who was then Foreign Secretary, accepted this reply as a refusal.—But Mr. Lincoln, among his very first acts, sent to England *an unconditional acceptance* of the clause for extinction of privateering. To the exceeding surprize of Mr. F. C. Adams, Earl Russell replied, that the right of privateering must be reserved for the South, whose belligerent rights we had recognized, but Mr. Lincoln was free to renounce it for the North.—Thus what was *"an inhuman practice"* while it was a strength to the merchant ships of the Union against England, becomes a natural and reasonable right, that must be revered,—as soon as it exposes the commerce of the North to the outrages of treasonable buccaneers.

In the same summer a large reinforcement was sent to Canada, which "The Times" explained, as intended to strengthen the province against Mr. Lincoln in certain contingencies. No one could suppose that *aggression* from him was feared. South and North alike interpreted it, that Lord Palmerston was preparing to attack Mr. Lincoln as soon as he thought it convenient. Indeed before long the English patronage of Southern privateers, who were supplied with coal, and sometimes feasted in English ports, went very far. These privateers at pleasure carried trained English sailors and the English flag, whether in the West Indies or in the English port of Nassau, most convenient for running the blockade. On one occasion when the privateer Nashville had taken shelter in the port of Southampton, and the Federal vessel Tuscarora lay off watching her, Lord Palmerston sent two English ships to intercept the Tuscarora, if she dared to move without allowing the Nashville twelve hours start. Favours of this sort to the South seemed ever to multiply as time went on.

No wonder that, in an earlier stage, when Commodore Wilkes boarded the English steamer Trent, and out of her took two Confederate Commissioners, Mason and Sliddell, general jubilee pervaded the North. Presently the

Crown Lawyers of England pronounced that *if* the Commodore had carried the ship . before an Admiralty Court in any maritime town for adjudication, he would have been blameless. But he had wished to spare the innocent passengers and the shipowners this vexation, and hereby unwittingly broke marine law. All Liverpool seemed to rejoice, and our Government Docks were set to urgent work. "The Times" gloated over imaginary conflicts with "the enemy." A deputation from the Friends' Society waited on Earl Russell, to remind him of the solemn engagement made by us in 1856, never in future to enter war without first seeking arbitration. The Earl alertly replied, that "this did not here apply, for *now* HONOR constrained us."—Honor ! the very point for which Arbitration was peculiarly suited. The Earl seemed to forget, how rudely and *arbitrarily* English captains had taken out of *neutral* American ships sailors whom America averred to be her own citizens ; and after peace with France, had formally reasserted her *right* to commit such outrage on a neutral power at pleasure.

Meanwhile President Lincoln, ignorant of our fuss and fury, had reproved Commodore Wilkes for acting on *English* principles that were *not* American ! and in hope of eliciting from us at length a disavowal of our old violences, sent a friendly dispatch, saying that the Commodore had acted *without instructions*, and any representations which her Majesty's Government might wish to make would be received with the most candid dispositions. Our war party had predicted that war was inevitable, because (they said) "the MOB in Washington would not allow the President to yield." But the *mob*, if anywhere, was in our West End Clubs, where the reception or presentation of any friendly dispatch was flatly denied ; *as if* Mr. F. C. Adams had forged the news. For three weeks Earl Russell allowed the controversy to go on,

when a word from him would have stopped it. Day and
night the work in the docks was as if war were imminent.
The public funds fell and great losses were sustained.
Shipowners could not get freights; a cutting peremptory
letter had been sent by Earl Russell wholely uncalled for;
yet after all, Palmerston got no pretence for war. In
America the President's decision was at once accepted;
and on December 27th his war-frigate St. Jacinto handed
over to the British authorities the much coveted but
superfluous gift of two oath-breakers.

In the first ten months Mr. Lincoln's navy-yards had
done wonders and his land forces multiplied proportion-
ally; but the *Confederates* were first to strike into the
navies of Europe a thrill of alarm, when the Merrimac
issued from Norfolk harbour into Hampton Roads (the
opening of the celebrated Chesapeake), to attack the
Northern ships' blockade. This fine vessel had been
seen and admired in European waters under President
Buchannan. The seceders had pulled up iron from their
railroads and roofed the ship with it, as well as casing
her. She proved unassailable to the Northern cannon,
while to them her shots were irresistible. Beneath them
a first-rate ship foundered with all her gallant crew. It
was at once discerned that England had no vessel that
could meet this ship hastily patched up, and the news
was unwelcome to the English war-party. Still more
unwelcome to them was the after-tidings. Next day
the Federal blockaders were suddenly reinforced by a
nondescript iron-cased vessel entitled the Monitor, small
and almost buried in the water, armed with one huge
gun that worked in an iron turret. A duel at once took
place, and after three hours of mutual battering, the huge
Merrimac was glad to scuffle away from her dwarfish
antagonist. We did not then understand the nature of
her distress, which was afterwards revealed to us in the

duel of the Fingal and the Weehawken, which I hope afterwards to detail. The Monitor gave a generic name to after-ships of the same build. Such vessels are admirable for defence inside a harbour, on smooth water, but frail against sea waves. The Merrimac was broken up by the Confederates to prevent her falling into the hands of the North; the Monitor foundered at sea when sent southward. Thus each had a short but brilliant life.

The next month (April, 1862) brought to Palmerston and Russell news still more funereal, and permanently altered their policy. Thenceforward they renounced the thought of *actual war* with Mr. Lincoln, at which they had before hinted as possible " in some contingencies." They now discovered that they might chance " to catch a Tartar," if they were too brave; for they suddenly learned that while an English Field Marshal, who had explored the defences of New Orleans, had been teaching us in *The Times* that capture of that city by the North was simply impossible, it was at that very time already captured. General Benjamin Butler had so dressed up his ships as to run past the fortresses unseen, and break through the chain. The Confederate army was glad to clear out before his land force of fifteen thousand men, carried in eighty vessels.

Palmerston vented his disgust by an impotent burst against General Butler, but undoubtedly learned, not only how absurd had been the confidence of our Ministry that the success of the North was *impossible*, but that the main probability of victory now lay on that side. The possession of the sea and vast naval superiority, with the recovery of New Orleans, assured to it the conquest of Louisiana. This was an evident augury of the whole war, and had been won in a single year; though Mr. Lincoln had begun without money, with empty arsenals and docks; while the traitors had carried off his money, his stores and his ships, and Palmerston had enabled them to get money, ships and ammunition from England. Yet English enmity did not at all abate. It is painful and tedious to give details, but readers may be referred to the speech of Charles Sumner (chairman of the Standing War Committee of the Senate), entitled "Our Foreign Relations." Suffice it here to say, that while our petting of *all* the Southern privateers was scandalous, in the case of the "Alabama" it manifested so gross connivance, and was so fatal to the merchant navy of New York (though in no respect influencing the war), that after the war the Royal Arbitrator laid on England an enormous fine: three millions sterling! The Alabama was destroyed as soon as the Kearsarge, a Northern war-ship, caught her. Another peculiarity must not be omitted. The Birkenhead shipbuilders seemed to wish to vie with both North and South by a new type of war-vessels, called *Rams*, in imitation of ancient Greek and Carthaginian ships, which manœuvred their brazen beaks to pierce the enemy. Lincoln's people were exasperated to white heat, and our Richard Cobden (I understand) was able to announce positively in England, that if our rulers allowed these rams to escape out of Birkenhead, Mr. Lincoln would interpret it as a declaration of war, and without further ado enter it actively against England and all her Empire. Certain it is, our Ministry quailed; just so did it in 1863, to Russia, the moment that Alexander II. had sent his Baltic fleet clear out of the Belts. Much foolish and disgraceful boasting as Whigs or Tories might encourage concerning the strength of the English Empire, yet Earl Russell did not need information from Cobden, that to defend every mile of our enormous sea-line was as pressing a point of "honor" as to resent the arrest of two perjured officials; and that merely to put our islands and Canada and Australasia into defensive trim against maritime attack, involves as much expense as would war itself to a commensurate continental power. Our overgrown Empire in every military sense assimilates us to *a hen with chickens*, not to an eagle.

Much as the Federate Americans dreaded these English *rams*, nothing came of one (off Alabama?) when they actually encountered it. Like a big galleon of the Spanish Armada, it could not turn so quickly as its smaller assailants, who avoided its shock, knocked it about side-wise, and without serious loss mastered it.

The tale now goes back to stout Benjamin Butler. On his return to Boston in 1864 he attested, that having of old been a "*Hunker* Democrat" (*i. e.* an out-and-out supporter of the South), he naturally took with him against New Orleans all "the *Hunkerest* Democrats" that he could gather. But when as Governor in and from New Orleans he set up legal tribunals and through them learned the horrible facts of social cruelty and foulness under slavery, its endurance seemed to deny any Divine Rule, and changed all his Hunkerest men, like himself, into pure Abolitionists. Such was the system, which an English Liberal Ministry, with the universal joy of the Tories and the mass of the London press, were eager to uphold. General Butler proved as sage an administrator, as (aided by skilled seamen) he had been a vigorous leader of the critical expedition. The capture of the city was such a surprize, that it involved no struggle. Against proud slave-holders and their insolent ladies (who were well aware in what an atmosphere of lust, rape, and incest their lives were passed), he maintained the rule of the North by the sacrifice of only two audacious lives. In that summer he for the first time freed the city from its habitual yellow fever by enforcing new cleanliness. He seemed to be precisely the man needed for his task; accustomed to civil rule, versed in law, anxious to order all things by law, yet capable of military severity against lawless plotters. To prevent the new growth of treason in a population of slave-holders, needed a resolute and energetic military governor.

His capture of New Orleans seems to have at once inspired the North with the hope of early success against Richmond, the capital of Virginia, where the Confederate Congress met, as the Federal Congress at Washington. The easiest passage towards Richmond seems *on our maps* to be along the higher level of Western Virginia, where the population consisted of free cultivators, mainly loyal to the Federals. But this route must have involved some military unfitness; for it was never contemplated. The second route would cross a series of rivers with steep banks and rapid courses nearly parallel; obviously very dangerous to a multitudinous army, which could nowhere cross in great mass, and when it had crossed, was liable to lose cohesion through swamps or brushwood, if not in forest; moreover it could ill foreknow where its enemy lay in force. An Englishman of high talent who had lived in Virginia, described to the present writer the extreme difficulties of that route, avowing his firm conviction that success by it was impossible to the North. A third route was far more plausible, because it enabled Mr. Lincoln to use his naval superiority; and it was embraced by Gen. Maclellan, whom, for reasons perhaps political more than military, the President then chiefly trusted. This route was to proceed towards the James's river, with powerful gunboats accompanying the army. Yet it might get entangled in the swamps of the Chickahominy; which, the Southerners had loudly boasted, were certain to be fatal to any Northern invaders. Any outside speculator might rather have expected the North to have cut off Richmond from her supports and from Texas the feeding-place of her armies, after Missouri and New Orleans were won. To this it came at last.

Maclellan went forth in vast strength by sea and by land. A series of obstinate combats followed, vaguely called the Seven Days' battle before Richmond : but the swamps of the Chickahominy were the truest cause of failure. He suddenly changed his head-quarters, apparently could not re-unite his vast array, and was forced to leave each scattered part to find its own way across the level peninsula (in close of July, 1862). North and South alike felt the very grave reverse, and the South now believed the season was come, at which they might hope to invade their invader.

Mr. Lincoln presently had to ask for 500,000 more troops which were at once voted to him by his Congress. We in England could not understand, indeed hardly could believe, his strong aversion to accept FREE Negroes of the North in the Federal Army. Under the sun of the South they were likely to be hardier than his white troops, while of their devotion to his cause and to African freedom no one could doubt. Probably when making so heavy demands on his white population, he at last felt that his refusal of coloured soldiers might cause dangerous disaffection : but instead of ignoring complexion, he separated the regiments and allowed smaller pay to the coloured. To go forward with this unpleasant topic, the stinginess of the nominal pay was not the worst part of the affair; but it gradually leaked out, that while his brave blacks were risking life or losing limbs for Mr. Lincoln, their families at home were starving because no pay was issued to the coloured troops; and this, not because the War Office was in any straits; for mere notes now passed as equivalent to gold. The blame may be cast on wicked subordinates; but nothing can excuse the President and his War Minister. At last the Chief Captain of these troops, a Mr. Stearns, indignant at the injustice, refused to lead them and laid down his commission. Disgrace was heaped on disgrace by the tidings, that *a special Act of Congress* was needed to compel the Executive to fulfil their guarantee and leave off their malicious fraud. I was slow to believe the fact and kept hoping for explanation, but none ever reached me. I fear to comment, and still try to hope that the newspapers deluded me. I have not been able to get denial of the facts.

The Northern generals had in reserve armies so large, that when Maclellan led away his shattered and out-worn force from the Chickahominy, Burnside, as new Commander-in-Chief, bombarded the city of Fredericksburg on the Rappahannock, the out-most river-barrier of Virginia, behind which the Confederate General Lee held watch. The attack was reckless in bravery; the Federals lost 7,000 men from their ranks, and Burnside evacuated Fredericksburg, after other large waste of Northern blood. Meanwhile Maclellan had re-inforced his army behind, and when Lee issued against him, each side was computed to draw up 100,000 men. The terrible battles of Antietam followed (September 14 and 15) by which Lee was said to lose 14,000 men, and Maclellan 12,500. Mr. Lincoln had already called for 600,000 volunteers, in two batches, in addition to the 500,000 troops voted to him by Congress.

A Richmond Professor named Jackson had taken arms for the South, and to distinguish him from other Generals of the same name, their army in compliment called him *Stonewall* Jackson. (Had he been asked, Are you fighting for Slavery? he would have answered, No! but for *State Right*. In this way the more specious Southerners justified themselves, as comfortably as any English soldier in this or that foreign aggression, by his plea, " I am fighting for *my country*.") This popular General was made chief of the invasion ; in Maryland Jefferson Davis counted to find warm local support. Mr. Lincoln expected the attack, and on September 22nd, *three days before* the actual invasion, issued a remarkable *contingent* proclamation, which, however illogical, delighted the friends of freedom everywhere, as marking a turn of the tide; which means, that Mr. Lincoln was taking a "new departure." His policy had hitherto been to soothe, to concede,—in hope of winning over the rebels by reserving for them their "slave-property." He now found them elated, hopeful, stronger and prouder. Did he despair of merely enticing them, unless he added a *threat?* Apparently : yet now less than ever were his threats likely to move them. Well ; he threatened, that *unless* they returned to obedience before the next New Year day, he would actually *declare* their slaves free !

What a guffaw of laughter must this threat have elicited from the defiant Confederates, to whom it came like a proof that only through conscious weakness he now betook himself to menace. They entered Maryland in great force. In one very fierce battle Stonewall Jackson was slain ; but Mr. Lincoln at length seemed tired of General Maclellan. The fatal January 1st, 1863, displayed the Confederates still very formidable, still unrepentant. Then Mr. Lincoln hurled his actual thunderbolt, no longer contingent, and proclaimed the slaves of the insurgent States to be free. The North collectively shouted applause. Charles Sumner carefully avoided one word of censure, and probably joined in congratulation. Wm. Lloyd Garrison presently boasted that the President had freed three millions of the coloured population. But Lord Palmerston commented sarcastically, " Mr. Lincoln sets free those who are not in his

power, and keeps in slavery those who are in his power."
I confess it was long before the conviction that Palmerston
had spoken, not mere sarcasm, but bitter truth, came to
me as a deadly stab. We learned the public facts in
fragments and believed newspaper summaries, which
often left us ignorant of details. The Proclamation of
Jan. 1st had iniquitous clauses, by which the President
excepted from freedom as many slaves as *he himself* might
choose to direct! So far as his reasons can be guessed,
he was aiming to please the loyalists of Upper Tennessee,
and to coax the disloyal in Louisiana. Whatever his
motives, in fact he kept in slavery the coloured people
of this *conquered* area, who immensely outnumbered those
liberated by him in North Carolina and elsewhere.
C. Sumner, Fremont, Hunter, and Phelps, would have
liberated the slaves in a rebel State, just as far as
Northern power reached, but with no further pretence.
What Mr. Lincoln might do, with a mind scrupulous,
pious, and puzzled, no one could foretell. His recall of
General Butler from Louisiana seemed at first mysterious,
but events explained it. Butler was too strong-minded
for Lincoln's coaxing of the disloyal rebels. He was
recalled on Dec. 16th, 1862, and superseded by General
Banks.—It may be named, that on the last day of that
year the original Monitor foundered at sea.

For another half-year the Confederate army obstinately
held its ground in Maryland, with no visible advantage.
Meanwhile Mr. Lincoln was every month stronger by sea,
and aspired to attack Charleston and Mobile (?). The
Confederates had left their women and old men to be
fed by the slaves, whose generosity and faithfulness was
wonderful in this time of distress. Moreover the demand
for arms, ammunition, uniforms, and general supplies to
the armies so pre-occupied them, that (it was told) drawing
room carpets were often cut up to make soldiers' blankets.

On the opposite side the North made no sensible abate-
ment of ordinary trade, and a vast increase in all
appliances of war. Its railways did work beyond
all precedent, so that (in spite of paper immensely
depreciated) English shareholders counted it a time of
prosperity. The Northern manufactories supplied everything in abundance; their farmers actively and with joy
sent agricultural supplies to the army. To crown all, we
are astonished to learn that during the whole war they
continued their arduous and rapid work at the first Pacific
Railway, as if it had been time of profound peace. Such
was the superior strength of the North, which Alexander
Stephens of Georgia correctly measured and vainly fore-
told. At length in July, 1863, on the first *five days*,
the great battles of Gettysburg were fought out between
General Meade for Lincoln and General Lee for the
Confederates. The South felt by the result, that its
resources were unequal to its enterprize. It had to fall
back on mere defence, disappointed, but still not con-
fessing its cause to be lost. Before these battles the
anxiety of the North had reached its worst: after that
crisis they felt that final victory was sure.

The date of a most interesting naval duel cannot be
here accurately fixed; but it probably comforted the
North just at its worst. To evade the English forms of
prohibition, English-built war-vessels were sent out without cannons or gunpowder; all the ammunition was
smuggled in what seemed like a merchant-vessel, with
iron rails as ballast. In this way a splendid ship called
the Fingal and built on the Clyde, ran through the
Northern blockade up a creek of North Carolina, whither
her armament soon followed her. But Mr. Lincoln's
navy-yards learned the fact, and sent two Monitors to
watch the mouth of this creek. The Southerners rapidly
and skilfully sheathed the Fingal with iron and expected

it to surpass the Merrimac. They gave it a new name, the Atalanta. Early in the grey of the morning one of the Monitors (called the Weehawken) got sight of a large vessel descending the creek. The Northern captain at once slipped his cables and ran out to sea, both to gain time of preparation and to notify the affair to his colleague. His little vessel had only one cannon, but the weight of its ball was four hundred and forty pounds! When ready for action he turned back to meet his antagonist singly, and boldly received shot after shot without damage, until he came conveniently near, directing the gun himself. When he had fired once, the Atalanta made no return. At his quickest convenience he repeated his shots, and after his fifth shot the Atalanta hauled down her flag and surrendered, before the other Monitor had time to join in the fray. Presently two large pleasure boats full of Southern ladies steamed down the creek, to see the glad sight of Northern discomfiture; but on finding the flag of the Atalanta struck, they turned back in hot haste to avoid capture. The crew of the Atalanta were so taken by surprize, that mere wonder subdued other feelings and made them garrulous. They fully explained their hopes and their plans, and the cause which compelled their surrender. To us also it explains, why the Merrimac failed in a duel with the Monitor; indeed it may now seem, that if the Monitor had known and trusted her own power, and had come closer to work, the Merrimac might have had the same fate as the Atalanta. For by the first shot from the Weehawken, the concussion made the guns of the Atalanta start from their places. Many of the crew were knocked down roughly. From the timbers, inside the iron sheath, big splinters flew out and inflicted ugly wounds. The gunners not only had to pick themselves up, but to get aid in replacing their guns; and before they were in gear to fire anew, the second shot from the Weehawken repeated the damage and again deranged their fighting. Of course pride retarded surrender; but the description makes one honor bravery which endured five shots before it learned that resistance was helpless and hopeless. That shots from the Atalanta which would have been fatal to any wooden antagonist, were without effect on the Weehawken, is to us equally amazing.

The Southern captives further explained, that they had fully counted on driving off their local guards, then to run along the coast and scatter all the Northern ships, and justify England in proclaiming the blockade broken; thus establishing their superiority on their own sea-coast. —But now, what a contrast! The *engines* of the Atalanta were not harmed, but she was sent northward, needing immense repairs. The Weehawken was sent southward to aid the blockade of Charleston, and anchored in the bay. But when a violent storm arose, her anchor pulled her under water, and she was lost with all her crew. Thus, like the Monitor, she performed for the North *one* brilliant deed; one only; then perished.

It is not amiss to add here some notice of the Civil action of the North in this first portion of the war, *i. e.* preceding the battles of Gettysburg. As each successive State issued its manifesto of secession, its representatives vanished from the Northern Congress,—all except one, Andrew Johnson, of Nashville, Tennessee. The previous repute of this man with Northern lovers of freedom was very low, but his singular adherence to the North *endeared him to Mr. Lincoln;* and the after-tale seems to allow, indeed suggests, a suspicion, that his secret influence with Mr. Lincoln was disastrous. Naturally the wide chasm of sentiment in the Congress between the Slave party and the Free party, with the habitual haughtiness of the former, constantly impeded legislation; but when the mass of the Southerners had cleared out, the Congress had a new freedom. It soon passed a *Homestead* law which previously was not possible : for, its object was to cover the soil with free cultivators and extirpate European pauperism, always apt to grow up from a landless population. The effect was also to sustain the rate of wages. The Congress successively made into free soil the area attached to Washington (called Columbia), likewise that of every Federal Fortress and Dockyard. They further passed a vote, authorizing the President to offer to Kentucky pecuniary aid to defray the loss contingent on liberating their slaves. But Kentucky preferred despotic power to money, and did not show herself at all grateful that her treasonable declaration of "neutrality" had not been punished.—More decisive still was the action against those official men who had violated their oath of allegiance to the Federal Government by active treason. In Europe they knew that all such traitors, if caught, would be hanged. They resolved not to imitate European Royalty. But for men who had laid on the Republic the strain and awful bloodshed of such a war, with the expense of millions of dollars,—how many no man yet knew,—confiscation of their land was a very mild punishment. Congress accordingly passed a bill to that effect; but as it had not a two-thirds majority the President could legally veto it ; and he did veto it ; so this time it did not become law. Here again he showed himself less wise than those over whom he was chief magistrate.

On the coast of North Carolina the naval superiority of the North had recovered a considerable tract with many thousands of slaves, whom Mr. Lincoln by his edict on January 1st, 1863, *declared free.* A philanthropic movement hastened from the North to help these freed men. The process was familiar, at least since the rush of the North to Kansas, to Missouri, to California perhaps. As a cardinal article for immigrants, where pine trees abound, circular saws are named, with other tools of the carpenter and mason; whatever is the most approved form of the plough, the cart, the harrow, &c., were quickly set up for the negro to imitate; next, flour mills, and better houses replaced mere huts or kennels, and in the second year, the freemen had schools of their own, with northern teachers, and, quickly, religious missionaries. Their old masters having vanished, the land seemed to be theirs. Alas! Mr. Lincoln's high-handedness emboldened his worthless successor to sweep back both the land, and all that they had built upon it, into the possession of the old masters.

When General Banks succeeded General Butler at New Orleans, the South was in full tide of success and pride, and it is not wonderful that neither General carried off any military "laurels." The President, in the very crisis of proclaiming freedom, showed to those who were cognizant of details, that his dominant idea was still, that upon *him* the coloured people had no rightful claim. We in England were very slow to believe the facts. It was in 1864 that I myself first learned the details of the new Constitution of Louisiana, set up by the sole personal will of Mr. Lincoln, and how firmly he enforced it. When some one hinted that it belonged to Congress, not to the President, to make a new Constitution for a rebel State; he replied: Congress may do as it pleases *after the war*: my arrangements are only *temporary* and for military necessity. But Mr. Lincoln, as military superior, had commanded General Banks to establish a local Parliament for which no coloured man should have a vote, while all the whites, unreconciled rebels, even those who had broken official oaths, should have the vote, on merely taking a new oath. This was an arming of rebels against his own Governor, in the midst of an unfinished war. Whenever unseen enemies are mingled locally in a city or country, patriotic men for the public safety gladly resign their own ordinary right. Surely in so dangerous a crisis a check of Congress on the President was far more needful, than after solid peace should be attained. In his resolve to show that he would not be dictated to, his acts of high power were a most dangerous precedent, and *Charles Sumner, hitherto self-repressed, was forced into open resistance.*

Little by little, with sore hearts, we learned how callous Mr. Lincoln was and that he claimed to play with slavery and freedom as cards at his disposal. But as regards *coloured freemen*, his dealing with *their* rights opened to us a new window into his mind. When I communicated my distress to certain friends, I got the reply: "Oh! that is all nonsense: surely you do not believe these lies of *The Times*: there is nothing about it in the *Daily News* or *Morning Star*." I could not accept this solution. The hostile papers could not invent the details: but the friendly papers were too much ashamed to tell them. It looked as if Mr. Lincoln had adopted the *dictum* of Judge Taney, "a coloured man has no right which a white man is bound to respect." History ought not to suppress this episode.

Mr. Lincoln bade General Banks to give the franchise to *all white* men and refuse it to *all coloured* men. Banks obeyed him; whereupon the *free* coloured men sent as deputation to the President two of themselves, gentlemen who had never been slaves, they nor their ancestors, making sure that he was unacquainted with facts, and never intended such injustice. He received them courteously and listened kindly to their words, which were to the following effect:

"Louisiana was not conquered by the U.S. but freely

ceded by Napoleon I. or rather sold under strict conditions, among which he required that the Union should
guarantee to all the existing residents (with no exception
of colour) the rights which they had enjoyed under
France.   Our ancestors, though coloured, were politically
equal to white men.   But after Louisiana had been made
a State of the Union, White Colonists kept flocking in,
and when their numbers made their vote irresistible, they
first voted the free coloured men out of the franchise;
next, made a Black Code for them, with special prohi-
bitions, special punishments and special processes of trial.
This breach of compact Napoleon I. (if he had lived and
been at leisure) might have taken up as a ground of war
against the Union.   Surely, Mr. Lincoln could not intend
to re-enact and re-establish this injustice."

The President replied, that their case was a very hard
one: he sympathized with them greatly; but *the laws of
Louisiana were sacred to him:* he saw *no military necessity*
why coloured freemen should vote: therefore he could
do nothing for them.—He did not even remember, that
as President his ordinary duty was to forbid in any
State the distinction of Privileged Orders.

Pressing military necessity was pre-requisite, that
Mr. Lincoln might overpower his sense of the sacredness
of an obviously iniquitous local law! Such was the
puzzled head and crooked conscience of the man selected
as Dictator in war and peace to a nation caught in a
terrible crisis.

Did the President not know how his phrase "coloured
men" would be interpreted in the whole Union? Had
he never read that Mr. Olmstead, correspondent of the
New York Herald, found that in Louisiana the grandchildren of white proprietors were whipped in the field?
Was he ignorant that masses of people called *Coloured*
were black, brown, yellow and white; some so white,

that only by examining the *areola* at the base of the thumb-nail any trace of the negro could be detected? Yet in a revolutionary crisis at which New Principles were to be established, he did his worst to nail down this arbitrary and unjust distinction of freemen into two classes, one privileged and dominant, the other degraded and subject.

The matter shocked the present writer so much, that he (foolishly as since appeared) wrote a letter of grief to Wm. Lloyd Garrison, who had boasted that Mr. Lincoln had freed three million slaves. I had always honored him (morally, not politically) and *intended* my address to be honorific. I certainly much displeased him: he, as certainly, fell much in my esteem. But I blamed myself for expecting sound judgment from one who had counselled to secede from the Union and abandon the slaves. I now counted him *a spent force*, and learned how wide his difference from Wendell Phillips as well as from Sumner.—Sumner resisted the President's dealing with Louisiana to the utmost in the Senate; and afterwards wrote to me, that if he could have counted on *six* men to support him, he might have effected something: but the fear of division in their ranks while the enemy was in the field, made the President master of the situation.

In England the friends of the South were helpless far too long. When Whigs and Tories join on any great question, their organs in the press take the same side, and the public is ill-informed as to the honest facts. Thoughtful and fair minds saw with half an eye that the question was between Slavery and Freedom; but very busy men learn foreign facts chiefly by their favorite newspaper. A new organ was needed. Thomas Bayley Potter, a rich man of Manchester, guaranteed needful money, others joined him, and "the Emancipation Society" quickly published a long series of instructive tracts.

Friends of the secession had made much of Mr. Lincoln's
fatuous announcement to Europe that the result of the
war would not affect the status of the slaves : but we
could not compliment on sagacity those who believed him.
Obviously, success of the South would direfully intensify
slavery, would presently re-open the slave-trade, would
variously humiliate and vex England ; while the success
of the North would force it *to take securities against a
recurrence* of such a struggle.   Two daily papers of
London adhered to justice and freedom, the *Daily News*
and *Morning Star*, and one weekly paper, *The Spectator ;*
but with large pecuniary loss !   Sir Charles Lyell for his
Geological researches had twice traversed the States ;
and knew their affairs well.   He and his wife were
forced to refuse invitations in London, and Lady Lyell
told me *why*.   The insults poured on them for wishing
well to the North made it hard to know how to behave :
the effort to suppress feeling threatened her with hysteric
attack.   Many less distinguished persons felt quite out of
place in a drawing room.   Such was still the London
atmosphere when the Emancipation Society met in the
summer of 1864, in hope of strengthening Mr. Lincoln's
heart, though not his hands.   The news concerning the
President's Louisiana Constitution could no longer be
doubted.   His whole policy showed itself worse and
worse.

Mr. Lincoln after a proclamation which presumed his
legal right to free the slaves on the rebel area, had shown
his determination to withhold the freedom at his own
convenience.   Western Tennessee, a vast nest of slavery,
had now been a second year in his power, might now
have solid freedom and be able to defend itself.   Yet
apparently in order to give hope to the rebels of retaining
their slaves, *(in spite of his nominal proclamation)* he
upheld slavery in Tennessee and in the greatest part of

Louisiana. It was now upheld, not as of old *sectionally*, by local State officers, but by the Federal Executive and by the arbitrary will of the faithless President, who refused to enforce his own gratuitous, long considered, solemn proclamation, in which he had prayed for the blessing of God, and the charitable construction of men. This was called by his English opponents "a villainous hypocrisy." What reply, alas! could we now make. The Georgian rebels were still armed, and they now knew what terms they could make, viz., *those which Mr. Lincoln dangled before them in Louisiana*. Let them even now propose peace, and he will avow that his own proclamation of freedom was *intended to be partial*, will declare the local laws of Georgia "sacred to him," will leave the coloured free men totally disfranchised, the slaves (at best) called serfs. The same will be true of nearly all the South. All the new freedom may be swept off by a reactionary policy, or indeed by new lawlessness if Mr. Lincoln thus cheats the ardor of the North, which has been kindled not only by zeal for the Union, but also by the memory of John Brown "whose soul is marching on" to victory, though "his body moulders in the grave." The President was under no duty to proclaim any man free who was not already under his power; but to issue the contingent proclamation (and some months later, the absolute proclamation), yet still limit it even against those actually in his power for two full years, was quite disgraceful.

TO THE EDITOR OF THE "ENGLISH LEADER."

September 1st, 1864.

Sir,—I am obliged to you for sending me a copy of Mr. Garrison's public reply to my letter, which I had not before seen. It puts me into a grave difficulty; for I do not desire any personal controversy: yet unless I disown his extraordinary misinterpretations of what I have written, I fear it will be supposed that I acquiesce in them.

My letter was not written for this side of the Atlantic, but for the Anti-Slavery and Republican party of the Union, who seem to me in danger of grave mistake in supposing Mr. Lincoln's *honesty* to be a vast advantage, and almost a security that things will come right. I am as much convinced of his honesty, I believe, as Mr. Garrison can be; and I distinctly say, when his principles are *not* those which an Anti-Slavery man should desire, the more honest he is, the worse for that cause. *He has been brave enough to veto the Congress in his tenderness for slave-holding rebels.* An eloquent gentleman from America defended to me the painful address made by Mr. Lincoln to the coloured men when he propounded his scheme for colonizing them, by saying that the President was only intending to throw dust into the eyes of the Kentucky slave-holders. I was shocked by that address, and ill accepted the excuse; but when his Emancipation Proclamation came, I thought he had turned over a new leaf. In a great national convulsion all is well that ends well; but it is now too manifest, that Mr. Lincoln has a mean prejudice against colour; and his public declaration that he greatly prefers gradual to sudden emancipation is no abstract preference, but is one which, in spite of his Emancipation Proclamation, he is bent upon making a reality, by introducing serfdom in place of slavery. Mr. Garrison totally misinterprets what I said was " a terrible truth;" although I wrote so explicitly as to think it impossible. The dry fact, stated without a particle of colour, is, that the President conferred freedom on the slaves of the States still in revolt, over whom he had no power; and refused to bestow freedom on the slaves of Tennessee and Louisiana *(after those States had revolted and had been subdued)*, over whom he had power. Nothing hindered him in the latter case but *his own interpretation* of the Constitution; which is *not* Sumner's interpretation, nor Butler's, nor Andrew's. I do not say that Mr. Lincoln is dishonest, as Mr. Garrison strangely supposes (and if I did think him dishonest, to impute publicly what I could not prove would be truly absurd and highly blamable): but I see his interpretation of the Constitution is such as to give vast advantage and vitality to the slave system; and from this I feel grave alarm for the future.

Mr. Garrison simply repeats the statement against which I remonstrated as clearly inaccurate, that the President emancipated more than three million slaves by his word; and still winks at the fact that he gratuitously sustains slavery in Tennessee, and did not abolish it on the Mississippi. He erroneously supposes that I regard the President to wield autocratic powers. It is not for me to define what are his powers; but as far as I have a right to have an opinion, it is, that Mr. Lincoln has exceeded his powers in his new and dangerous Louisiana Constitution. Native Americans must look to such matters. I look only to great moral interests. Undoubtedly I do expect, that, if he is to have any honor from us, he shall treat the coloured race as his "fellow-citizens," and shall recognize in them, wherever he has legal power, the same rights which any ordinary European, *any English Tory nobleman*, would recognize. It is notorious that English generals regarded the revolt of the American colonists as a forfeiture of their right to have their local laws respected; and therefore, as a thing of course, saw in their slaves only men and not property. Mr. Lincoln insists, to this day, on seeing the slaves of Tennessee as "property;" and I cannot make Mr. Garrison understand that I am shocked to find *him* (Mr. G.) not to resent this. It is a simple fact, and not an imputation on my part, or an "unmerited sarcasm," that Mr. Lincoln does *not* regard the treason of the rebels to have forfeited their local rights over their slaves; but does regard present and galling danger, and that alone, to justify his emancipation; and after nominally emancipating, he does his best (or his worst) to hinder the emancipation from being sudden; *i.e.*, to keep the coloured race in serfdom under exasperated whites.

I earnestly trust that the Congress will overrule this. If it do not, I have a mournful certainty that long and chronic miseries will convulse the Union, and will endanger the safety of what seems to have been won. European intervention will follow any renewal of war. This also Mr. Garrison passes over, as if I had not said it. He once more blows a trumpet note to Mr. Lincoln, and shuts his eyes to the possibility that this frightful scheme of serfdom may yet ruin everything.

I saw in another paper an extract from Mr. Garrison, which I do not see in this letter, where he pleads the non-enfranchisement of English peasants as justifying Mr. Lincoln in refusing to allow political suffrage to the coloured race of Louisiana. Besides all the other cardinal diversities of the cases, this overlooks that Mr. Lincoln has volunteered to put the coloured race there *beyond the protection of Congress*, and has put them back into the local power of the white men who had already cruelly oppressed them, who also revolted in order to continue that oppression; white men who had broken the treaty with France by which the rights of the coloured freemen in Louisiana were secured. Surely even Mr. Lincoln's duty to France is here something.

F. W. NEWMAN.

When the Emancipation Society in London actually met, a member was anxious that in our address to Mr. Lincoln we should incorporate some expression of grief at his respecting the unjust enactments of a rebel state, or else, send no word of thanks and approval. No actual debate and voting took place; all was stopped by the utterances of a very influential man, who in heart must have agreed with Sumner. He pronounced that any remonstrance with the President would be an insult. That man was John Bright, since "The Right Honorable."—A statesman is seldom expected to rise above "Expediency," yet Charles Sumner was a statesman, every inch of him. He never swerved from Justice, and never found Justice inexpedient.

After the South retired from Gettysburg, the struggle for Vicksburg, a fortified city on the Mississippi, had chief interest. Countless brave Northerners, black and white, were repulsed in numerous attacks, slain or crippled; Grant and Sherman being the Northern leaders there prominent. When at last it fell, Grant was again at work on the fatal Virginian rivers. Sherman soon was master of Atalanta, chief city of Georgia, and quiet observers discerned that in a military sense the rebel cause was now lost. The Southerners lamented that they had always one army too few in the field. Sherman swept across to Charleston, without meeting a foe, and by demolishing the railways which fed Lee's army in Virginia brought victory nearer. But to overcome Southern obstinacy, Grant had to endure vast carnage, before Richmond itself fell into his hands. The army under Lee escaped, but Sheridan the active leader of the Northern cavalry, soon overtook it, and forced it to surrender. April 9th, 1865, is remembered as the day on which Lee finally yielded at the Appomattoc Court House. Almost an exact four years completed the dreadful war. What a flea-bite to England was her enforcement of freedom in the West Indies and elsewhere with mere payment of money, compared with this wondrous heroism and life-sacrifice of democratic Americans. Pity that our Prince Albert did not live to see how a free *Republic* would conduct a great war!

General Sherman had no sooner entered Charleston than the blacks and coloured men held a public meeting and put together money for a School Fund. Such was their eagerness to learn and to teach.

To us the main interest in this cardinal struggle is *the moral dealing :* therefore the narrative must resume civil affairs in the North. The Congress on re-assembling enacted anew the confiscation of landed estates for all perjured officials, by a majority now so large that the President had no legal veto. Hereupon Mr. Lincoln brought back to them their law duly signed by himself, presenting it with words to this effect : " Official duty has compelled me to add my signature : but I intend to disobey the law, whenever I see disobedience to conduce to the public welfare." This utterance naturally and justly moved deep indignation. One member of Congress commented : " For taking on himself to break an Act of Parliament, James II. was ejected from the crown of England : and now our President tells us, that this is the way he is ready to serve *us*." But still the Congress dreaded to quarrel with the President while war confronted them.

What are men's motives we oftenest have to guess ; but that Lincoln was stirring vehement discontent, Andrew Johnson must have known, and the crisis enabled him to take the shine out of Lincoln and earn political capital as one thoroughly in earnest for freedom. He did not lose the opportunity of a deed unimagined in boldness. He issued from Nashville in Tennessee

an edict, saying that *like the President*, so *he*, Andrew
Johnson, takes on himself to proclaim freedom, and
hereby sets free all the slaves in Tennessee. We in
England rejoiced and were amazed. No doubt Lincoln
learned that if he was to be made President for another
four years, he must not let Andrew Johnson take the
wind out of his sails. He sincerely desired a *gradual*
not a *sudden* liberation, (this was W. Lloyd Garrison's
justification of him to me, as if I had doubted his sin-
cerity) but it seems he at last saw that the tenderly
cherished system had got its death-wound. Somehow,
soon after this, we heard that Lincoln was a candidate for
renewal of his Presidency, and that freedom was to be
universal.

In old Rome was a good law, that no officer who held
elections could himself be a candidate; indeed ordinarily
re-election in the very next year was disapproved, lest a
high officer use public time and official power less for the
public good than in intrigue for his own continuance in
power. Not even when public danger called for a Dictator,
could the Dictator's term be prolonged. But in the autumn of
1864 the American *election* of a President became nominal,
being really dictated by and for Mr. Lincoln, unless our
accounts are very deceptive. He zealously pleaded that his
own re-election was commanded by prudential necessity,
because *it was unwise to swap horses in crossing a stream*.
To us, East of the Atlantic, it was not at all clear what
mischief or danger would follow, if Lincoln, who always
had to learn by the disasters of the North, were succeeded
by one of Charles Sumner's school, who have fixed and
trustworthy principles because not variable uncertain
Expediency, but Right is their fixed and guiding star. But
the more Mr. Lincoln saw his past errors, naturally the
more he hoped to retrieve them in a second term of four
years. Ah! if he had but stuck to his own theory,

of "not swapping" in a dangerous crisis. But while Lincoln voted Lincoln into continued office, the same Lincoln voted against re-electing his long proved and trusty Vice-President; and being deep in self-conceit, but shallow of mind, *swapped* him for the unproved, untrusty schemer Andrew Johnson. By this unfaithfulness to his own doctrine, Lincoln in dying by the hand of an assassin, gratuitously bequeathed to the coloured race a new well of miseries not yet dried up.

The Unionists of the South had previously felt that after peace should be re-established and the armies of the North withdrawn, there would be no quiet for them, no public career, perhaps no security, if the whites still disloyal were masters of the local legislature. Only from political power in the hands of coloured men could life in their native States be endurable. When they pressed this fact on those Northerners whose trade is politics, they were shocked to find how cold and unsympathizing were this cautious clique. But with Mr. Lincoln when he entered Presidency for the second time the case was different. With him the safety of *white* men seems to have been as pressing as "military necessity." Their danger swept aside all the obvious objections to illiterate voters. The coloured race were sure to be staunch zealots for the Union, and a useful balance against the disaffected; and in a few years they would all be readers. Therefore the President resolved, that the *freed-men* must be made *full citizens*, and must have the ballot as a safeguard of their own rights. But on what moral ground should the change be based? An obvious reply was, On the doctrine of THOMAS JEFFERSON, who entitled the slaves *citizens and brothers*. Then a Declaratory Law would suffice, if merely enunciated by Congress, as interpreting the Declaration of Independence. This would suit Charles Sumner admirably, but it could not please

Mr. Lincoln; for it would condemn his whole conduct to the coloured race from first to last. He insisted on an Amendment of the Constitution, an elaborate and lengthy process, which on the rebel area could only be carried by military terrorism; that is, by the slave party not daring to impede the vote while victorious armies were still in mental view. This method, it may seem, was natural to the policy which demanded an Act of Congress to enforce issuing of pay to dark-skinned soldiers. But the President's strong will prevailed, and by an Amendment of the Constitution coloured men had equal votes with whites. But they were left destitute and landless, defrauded of their past life's wages.

Mr. Lincoln well knew how addicted the South was to Lynch law, how inveterate their contempt of the black, brown, yellow race, and of all who show a trace of African blood; how accustomed also to fire-arms and bowie knives and guerrilla under any captain; how helpless on the contrary were the freed-men as to all combination for defence. If a Fremont had been consulted, it would have been obvious to organize the freed-men into a militia, and train them; plenty of crippled Northern soldiers were equal to this task. But Lincoln did not even move for securing to the men whom he had, years before, pronounced free, a legal right to the houses, mills, workshops, schools, chapels, which their own labour, aided by Northern philanthropy, had erected, nor to the land on which these stood. On the contrary, by avowing his own readiness to over-rule a just Act of Congress, he unawares emboldened his successor to lawless injustice, and to forgive, where Congress had condemned. It is a cruel tale. Instead of buying the greatest result from the patriotic blood so lavishly poured forth at his call, he cheated his heroes of their reward to the utmost of his power, and in the rebel States perpetuated the old virus under the sons of the old tyrants. The coloured race gained the nominal franchise, but under fear of the white man's pistol have to vote as he bids them.

Can this too powerful President ever have seriously studied for the welfare of the four millions whom he so reluctantly declared not to be rebel-*property?* So gentle and religious a nature cannot have frankly avowed to himself the creed widely imputed by malignants to the North: viz., "I hate slavery politically, as a curse to white men; but for men of darker hue, I have neither pity, duty nor care."—Yet his conduct may seem to utter this creed dumbly.

Mr. Lincoln deserved no hatred, and if not respect, yet certainly thanks, from the fanatic who murdered him. His martyrdom cast a shroud over his very grave faults, and stabbed the North to its heart. We never *know*, whether greater wisdom in a ruler would without convulsion and anguish have really gained the good results sought; but when we see the mischiefs of misrule, we have only to bow submission. God's Kingdom certainly will come; but Man himself pays the price, most lavishly, —hitherto: *why*, the Nations themselves have to discover.

As brute animals set before mankind many striking lessons of temperance and content, so do rude tribes of mankind sometimes exhibit to our conceited Civilization signal lessons of Justice. As to this matter of Slavery the native American tribes, which by the policy of the slave-holding States of the Union were settled in the Indian Reserves, had imported from their powerful white neighbours the idea and the institution of human slavery. But when they heard that President Lincoln had proclaimed freedom to all the slaves, and was waging a great war for freedom, a war which soon after was crowned with victory, they themselves reconsidered the institution, and imitated the "Great Father" at Washington, by freeing all their slaves. But unlike President Lincoln, and *unlike the English Parliament of* 1833, they at once understood that the freed-men must not be left destitute and landless. Therefore, as though it were an obvious morality that free men and fellow citizens had an equal right with themselves to the land given to all alike by God, they *re-divided* their own plots, and gave equal portions to those newly freed. Thus the morality of barbarians, as of unsophisticated young folk, is sometimes a lesson and a reproof to experienced world-hardened statesmen.

1889. Into what new convulsion is the noble American Union now drifting? Years have passed since its Minister in London told us, that when a coloured deputation complained of being threatened with white men's pistols whenever the ballot boxes were to be filled, THE PRESIDENT of the Union replied, that " if the coloured men had not courage to maintain their own rights, he regretted it, but could not help them." Such was the London rumor; and that the Minister *did not see* such a reply to be an exhortation to local war! In 1861 the coloured race was called *four* millions; it is now reckoned at *nine* millions; and they are " boycotted," not in the South only. A coloured governness from Pennsylvania, the Quaker State, came lately to this town, attesting that even there no one would give her the *lease* of a house, in which she might teach coloured girls. That is the smallest part of the persecution. Efforts are made to exclude all who are judged "coloured" from all knowledge, and from any but the meanest and worst paid occupations. The dominant race treat them as Indian Pariahs, however light their complexions or high their natural abilities. Texas never saw the Northern armies; that in thát State the whites should be audacious, and the coloured race should barely know their own rights, is less wonderful. But the most heinous scandal is, that in some Southern States, laws have been passed imposing penal servitude on inter-marriages! and such laws are cruelly enforced; a fact notorious to the Federal authority, which is meekly trying to soothe and persuade men who are tyrannical brutes, that it would be *their interest* to behave more kindly. A FEMALE PRESIDENT would quickly become champion for *white women* whose beloved husbands these white tyrants are re-enslaving as felons. But when the oppressed race has become twelve or fifteen millions, perhaps even *our stupid sex* will see the deadly reefs ahead into which the shallow Expediency of Abraham Lincoln has legitimately piloted the Union.

PART IV.

THE GOOD CAUSE OF PRESIDENT LINCOLN.

A LECTURE PUBLISHED BY THE EMANCIPATION SOCIETY,
APRIL, 1863.

THE people of the Free States of North America have in this war for the supremacy of Law over Lawlessness risen to a patriotic self-devotion to which nothing known to me in English history can compare, except the spirit in which the English yeomen and townsmen resisted the tyrannical attempts of Charles I. The sympathy of the English millions with the cause of the North has been again and again solemnly recorded in the three first months of this year, and it will undoubtedly aid to nerve and sustain the Northern resolve. But besides this, it does our own hearts good to sympathize with a just cause, and with men who are sacrificing self for noble ends. Perhaps our highest idea of God himself is that of One always and everywhere loving Righteousness and rejoicing in the Just. We ourselves earn some portion of the divine joy, when our hearts go out in warm affection to a good cause solely because it is good.—How wicked are the aims of the South, I need not here insist; but how good and wise has been the aim of President Lincoln and of the great party which raised him to power,—has not been at all adequately set forth in this country. Englishmen have put the Union into contrast with freedom, and have actually made it out to be a guilt to fight for the Union; while really to fight for it is to fight for Law, for Nationality, for Civilization, for ultimate freedom to All, against sheer Barbarism, Lynch Law, and despotic unlimited crime.

For the forty years which preceded 1860, the Free States had endured the reproach of Europe for neglecting their duties to the enslaved negro. Nor only so; but through an instinctive dread of the convulsion which has now overtaken them, they shrank from too rude a shock with the encroaching Slave Power, and made concession after concession, which, even when they did not strengthen the adversary, yet puffed him up with pride and fresh audacity. A main reason of moral weakness in the North was, that they did not know their duties: and no nation of industrious men will ever willingly take up a war in which they are to bleed, except from a sense of duty. All Europe has carped at the Union, as implicated in the guilt of slavery; but the millions of the North imagined, that as the Free States had no power by the law to alter Southern Institutions, therefore they had no responsibility. Europe replied: "Not so; it is true that you cannot do *all;* but by law you can do *some* things. Do all that you can, and power will come to you to do more."—But it needed much exhibition of illegality, ferocity and unscrupulousness on the part of the South, before the North could learn how vital was the necessity for resisting the Slave Power. The cause of their dulness lay in the Constitution itself, which left the relation of the slaves to the Federal authority very indefinite. At this we cannot wonder, when the framers of the Constitution expected slavery soon to die out, and did not wish to recognize it *at all.* From the mere words of the Constitution one may reason to opposite results: nevertheless there is decisive proof in its historical development, that Southern statesmen regarded the slaves to be, equally with white men, *direct subjects of the Federal Common-*

wealth. This is demonstrated beyond question, by the liability of negroes to serve in the Federal army. When an English fleet, in the war of 1812-1815, invaded New Orleans, General Jackson pressed slaves into his ranks against us. Many of them were killed : but neither the Congress nor President Madison (a Southern President) would listen to the demand of the masters for remuneration; nor was any further appeal made. Thus was settled historically and *ex post facto* the place of the Southern negroes in the Commonwealth. They are called in the Constitution " persons held to service," not *chattels;* and by practical fact we see that they are not accounted foreigners, are not persons outside of the Union, but are *its subjects*, who owe to it warlike duty with the risk of their lives. Thus to the Federal power they were as minors in a family, or as women,—without direct political rights, yet still members of the political community, owing loyalty, and therefore claiming protection. Out of this position of things rose the obscure problem, What were the Free States to do ? How were they to protect the negroes from cruel local laws and lawlessness?

A solution was devised by an English Bishop, and solemnly approved by an Archbishop who was himself a Political Economist, no less a person than Archbishop Whately of Dublin, who has recently published the scheme anew in his reply to Mrs. Beecher Stowe's letter. This solution of the problem was, to impose an *ad valorem* tax on slaves, after allowing the owners to fix the values ; and then empower the Federal Government to purchase any slave or slaves at that price, whenever convenient. Unfortunately this Archiepiscopal plan was just as practicable as the rule for catching a sparrow by putting salt on its tail. The slave-owners were resolved that slavery should not be terminated. Had they been willing, there were many ways of effecting it, as the experience of the Spanish colonies showed. But they did not choose to fix prices, nor to submit to a tax, nor to do anything with the view of overthrowing a system which they fanatically glorified and were struggling to extend. We cannot wonder at the arrant nonsense and injustice printed and talked from end to end of England, when an experienced Economist, Politician and Peer could deliberately recommend such a scheme, even after actual trial had shown that the slave-holders of the still loyal State of Kentucky refuse to accept from Congress the pecuniary aid it offers to gradual emancipation.

A second solution of the problem has met wonderful favour with those who seem above all things to desire a break-up of the Union, while they profess to seek the benefit of the slaves and the interests of philanthropy. It is simply this : that the Free States should *peaceably separate* from the Slave States, and thus liberate their own consciences.—I must beg you to attend in detail to all that is involved in this much applauded scheme. *First*, in no case could it have done any good to the slaves, but must have made their prospect more hopeless than ever. The South has but now rebelled, expressly in order to secure undivided controul over itself;—in order to keep down free speech, free writing and free thought concerning slavery *even among white men called free*. It declares that slavery cannot be maintained otherwise. In order to intensify and extend the horrible system,—to have its hands unfettered for renewing the African slave trade as soon as it pleases, (by stealth, if not legally) and shut out the action of the Northern mind,—it has seceded. And now, forsooth, the friends of the slave advise, as if in the interest of the slave, to let the South go and work its wicked will, unmolested by any rights and duties of the North, and even by moral suasion. What else would this have been on the part of the North, but a cowardly dereliction of duty? And this, it seems, is the way in which the North is *to liberate its conscience!* But *secondly*, it must have been treason, not only to the negroes, but to the industrious portion of the Southern Whites, who do but endure the system of Slavery, while they have interests wholly, and inclinations generally, adverse to it. Look to the map and see how the Alleghanies run southward. Their slopes are unfit for slave-culture and are tilled by freemen. Western Virginia, Eastern Tennessee, the mountain land of the two Carolinas, of Georgia, of Alabama,—and even a portion of the State of Mississippi is in like case. Maryland and the Chesapeake Bay have loyal Unionists of the same character—industrious peasant farmers. The great State of Missouri had a larger mass of industrious whites than of slaves: so perhaps had Texas. If the North had seceded, it would have cast most unjustly upon these men the whole battle against slavery, into which they would inevitably have fallen, as indeed the Hon. Mr. Spratt of South Carolina distinctly intimates; but the freemen of the mountains must have been crushed by the planters and by the idle whites who are their tools. But *thirdly*, without a Fugitive Slave Law peace would have been impossible. The North, after secession, would have had to maintain great armies in defence of the vast frontier, over which fugitive slaves would have been pursued by marauding hunters. But if the Northerners consented to give back fugitives, they would once more be implicated in sustaining the guilty system, and their secession would fail of its supposed object. In fact, it shows the shallowest understanding of the case, to imagine Peace under Disunion possible between powers so intensely unlike as a North loving freedom and a South fanatical for slavery. War must have been chronic between them, while living side by side, with countries interpenetrating and rivers running across them. But *fourthly*, what is more decisive still, the North could not *secede peaceably*. The Southern planters would rather rule the Union than separate, though they would rather separate than be ruled. A Slave Empire is their darling idea, the goddess of their adoration. If New England and the North West had tried to " secede peaceably," while the Executive Power of the Union was wielded by the South, the President would have crushed the movement with a high hand, as lawless and treasonable. All the Slave-States, all the Democratic Party of the North, would have sided with the Union, and thereby with the Slave-Power. Illinois, Indiana and Ohio certainly, Pennsylvania, New York and even Connecticut probably, would have gone with the South. The seceders must have been subdued in the attempt, and the Slave-Power would have moved many degrees northward. In short, the attempt *to run away* from the responsibilities of the Union would have been more foolish than a direct crusade to liberate the negroes: for it would have entailed the same war, but in a more ignominious and less hopeful form ; having no elevating moral principle, no chance of rallying Southern lovers of freedom, no possibility of arming strong negro regiments, no claim of recognition by European powers. It would have surrendered the Capitol and its traditions to the enemy, and have taken pains to put itself into the wrong with all the world. Yet this most stupid, unpractical, cowardly scheme of abandoning responsibilities is to this day vaunted and held up in England as that which was the duty of the North ;—that of which it ought, even now, before it is too late, to accomplish a fractional part. The professed friends of the slave among us implore the North not to conquer *all* the Gulf States, but to leave at least *a little* independency !— forsooth an independency devoted to glorify slavery, for the curse of its neighbour and of the civilized world.

I unwillingly confess that this scheme once,—that is, in the long days of *despair and disgust*,—found advocates in that small, very devoted, very useful and noble-hearted band of enthusiasts, properly called Garrisonians, whom many of us are apt to identify with Abolitionists. I honour and esteem highly these martyrs to freedom. They gave the first great moral impulse to the glorious struggle now in progress; yet I cannot defend them from the charge of fanaticism. They certainly did not understand politics as did Charles Sumner and Henry Wilson, the senators from Massachusetts. The Garrisonians are moralists,—prophets, if you please; not statesmen; and have been unable to understand the difficulties of statesmen. What is still more to the purpose, their conduct in the present crisis shows that nothing but *sad despair* ever made them talk of secession. Their most eloquent leader Wendell Phillips, within a week of Mr. Lincoln's first call for troops, seeing the enthusiasm of the country, went into the war with all his heart. So too did Garrison; who not long back wrote to a friend in England his wonder that any friend of freedom could fail to sympathize warmly with the North in a war which will beyond all doubt extend freedom from the Lakes to the Gulf of Mexico, from the Atlantic to the Pacific. Previously, the Garrisonians were vehement and invaluable preachers against slavery, and brave helpers of fugitive slaves, with enormous losses and risks to themselves; but they did not propound any political scheme for abolishing slavery. In fact, they declined all political action; hence to call them Abolitionists is misleading. They did the work of their day: let us honor them for it; but it is now past. But the Republican Party of the North adopted a *practical political* course, and are justly entitled

Abolitionists by the Southern press and the Southern manifestoes. They maintained, that, having been born in the Union and having enjoyed under it countless blessings, their duty was to cling to it and to use *constitutional* means of correcting whatever was amiss. All such means were *either*, by the political action of the Federal Government, whether executive or legislative, *else* by moral persuasion directed towards the whites of the South, who alone had legal power to alter the local laws. For the former they wanted a President devoted to freedom, also a majority in the Senate; for the latter they wanted a suppression of every form of mob-rule and lynch law, which crippled peaceful suasion and stopped free speech and free press in the South. For this suppression again was needed a President energetically on the side of law and right.

The spirit and purpose of the Republican leaders is well summed up in the following passage of a speech of the Hon. Henry Wilson, senator from Massachusetts, and Chairman of the Military Committee of the United States:—He says:

"Abhorring slavery in every form, loving equal and impartial liberty for all men, I am ever ready to exercise *all the powers of the Constitution* of our country to relieve the nation from all connection with and all responsibility for slavery. . . and I am also ready to use *all means sanctioned by law, humanity and religion* to persuade our countrymen of the slave-holding States to undo the heavy burdens and let the oppressed go free. But I am *utterly opposed to all appeals*, by whomsoever made, *to force and violence*. Ours is a Government of Constitutional Law,— a Government of the people for the people. Not therefore to the rifle or the pike should the friends of the slave appeal, but to the heart, the conscience, the reason and the enduring interests of the people of the Slave States, upon whom rests the responsibility of Slavery in the States."

Is it not a slander to say, that men who hold these noble sentiments are not friends of freedom, *merely because* they utterly deprecate selecting War as the appropriate means of promoting it?

But the question arose: Supposing a President to be elected (as Mr. Lincoln was elected) by the votes of the party of Freedom, what steps could be taken in accordance with the Constitution for the benefit of the negro? This has been so little set forth in England and is so little understood, that it deserves notice here. The fact is, that there was everything for the enthusiasts of freedom to hope, everything for the fanatics of slavery to fear. The alarm of the South was expressed aloud in every State manifesto, and was evidently unfeigned. Nothing can be more decisive than the address of South Carolina on taking the first step:

"Responsibility follows Power; and if the people of the North have the power by Congress to promote *the general welfare* of the United States by any means which they deem expedient, why should they not assail and overthrow the institution of slavery in the South? *They are responsible* for its continuance or existence *in proportion to their power.* Experience has proved that slave-holding States cannot be safe in subjection to non-slave-holding States. . . . . The people of the North have not left us in doubt as to their designs and policy. United as a section in the late Presidential Election, they have elected as the exponent of their policy one who has openly declared that the States of the Union must be made all Free States or [all] Slave States. It is true that among those who aided in his election there are various shades of anti-slavery hostility. But if African slavery in the Southern States be the evil which their political combinations affirm it to be, *the requisition of an inexorable logic must lead them to emancipation.* When it is considered that the Northern States will soon have the power to make the SUPREME COURT what they please, *what check can there be* on the unrestrained counsels of the North *to emancipation?"*

It is needless to quote further; but I add the opening words of the manifesto from Louisiana on seceding:—"Whereas it is manifest, that Abraham Lincoln, if inaugurated as President of the United States, *will keep his promises to the Abolitionists,* which will *inevitably lead to the emancipation* of the slaves of the South," &c.,—therefore Louisiana resolved to secede. Englishmen have strangely disbelieved alike what the South and the North have said on this matter; and yet all is very plain. The short of it is this. So ruinous, so immoral, so impure, so hateful to humanity is that worst form of slavery which the Southern planters have hugged to their heart, that it would soon fall before free speech and free press, if these were maintained. This the planters well knew. Jefferson Davis indeed [now President of the South] distinctly claimed that the North should have no beliefs about slavery that were unpleasant to the South. Without tarring and feathering of white men, without house-burning, assassination and lynch law, such slavery *as that* is untenable. With a free press the poor whites of the South would soon learn that the system is their degradation, and would overthrow it. In order to keep up lynch law and popular violence against the free speech of *white* men, a President was needed, who should abuse the powers of his high office.—Yet it is well also to mention in detail, what might have been done against slavery by President Lincoln, even if the South had remained in the Union.

First, even unsupported by the Legislature, the President himself could enforce the law against African slave-traders, *could declare free coloured men to be citizens of the Union,* could liberate all slaves who were taken by their masters into a Territory [that is, into a District of the Federal Division which had not yet State Rights], could enforce faithful delivery of letters and newspapers from the Post-offices (a very important point) and could do much, if not everything, to defend speakers and preachers from the violence of lawless mobs. His *patronage* also has much weight with the poor whites of the Slave States.

My friend Mr. Francis Pulszky, who with Kossuth visited all parts of the Union, informed me in 1853 after his return, that Southern leaders had avowed to him, exactly as had the Northerners, that if the President's Cabinet were permanently in the interests of freedom, *the poorer whites might ere long outvote the planters in their own States.* In Missouri they did so several years back, and much was there to be hoped; of which indeed we now see the fruits. But the Southerners, to meet the danger, have since baited the idle class of poor whites in the Gulf States with the promise of cheap slaves from Africa; and as it seems, with much temporary success.

But secondly, as soon as the President could count on a majority in the Senate [or Upper House of Congress] his power would be immensely increased. He was sure to be able to do the very things which he has now done; to recognize Hayti and Liberia, and receive black ambassadors; make treaty with England for mutual right of search in order to stop the slave-trade; free the district of Columbia on which Washington stands;—we may add, free all the arsenals, forts, navy-yards of the South, in which Congress has exclusive jurisdiction. The *intention* to do all this was imputed to Mr. Lincoln confidently by the South in their manifestoes.

Now this majority in the Senate might be counted on at no distant day, for by Northern colonization one and another Territory were to be admitted as Free States, while the Southerners, having *no immigrants* and only half the population of the North cannot people new territories so quickly: or, if they did, the President would be able to declare their slaves free, as fast as they came in, and enforce their freedom. Moreover, the number in the Senate depends on the number of States. Likewise there was hope that Delaware, Maryland and even Missouri might soon become Free States; Virginia before long, and after it Kentucky. Different minds will form different estimates, of such probabilities. Suffice it to say that the North hoped this, the South dreaded it, and there were causes in action tending this way. Besides what is on the surface, it may be named that a Society had been formed in the North for colonizing Virginia by buying up large tracts of land and sending in freemen enough for self-defence. Western Virginia is wholly unfit for slave-culture, but very valuable to industrious freemen: Eastern Virginia is largely abandoned; old fields have long run wild from wasteful treatment and tobacco crops. Slave-breeding has superseded slave-labour; and there is ample room for freemen who can make a garden of that which is a desert under the forced work of slaves. With Western Virginia more than half free already and warmly attached to the Union, any large immigration would make it easy to an energetic President to support free discussion and a free press against local violences. Every step in this direction would be sure to give new impetus to the influx of freemen; nor was it at all wild to hope that the free cultivators who were not slaveholders might at an early period carry laws to ameliorate slavery. If they had begun even to *discuss* many delicate topics,—such as the *right* of a State-legislature to reduce a class of men to slavery (say, red-haired men, squinting men or woolly-haired,—or its right to define whether Mulattos are, or are not, negroes),—the free discussion itself would have shaken slavery to its foundation. Nearly the most disgusting atrocity of the American institution to white men, is the selling away to strangers as a slave the child of a white father, her own father perhaps getting a large price for her beauty! Any discussion opens at once the question of *fact*, Is a Mulatto or a Quadroon a negro? and the question of *right*, Ought the Inter-State slave trade to be tolerated?

The Inter-State trade was judged by Lord Macaulay to be even more atrocious than the African slave trade. The intention to stop it was deliberately charged against Mr. Lincoln by the Convention at Mobile. There is great uncertainty on this question as to the *powers* of the Federal Government, which certainly is empowered "to regulate Commerce" among the several States. *If* the North would accede to the Southern theory that negroes ought to be classed (as they phrase it) "with jackasses and nutmegs," Congress would have legal right to stop the trade in negroes as *chattels*. But the North treats them as "persons held to service," in fact as part of a family, which bars its right of forbidding their migration. But from the day that the Senate had any permanent majority for freedom, the right of this cruel trade was sure to be questioned; and when the Supreme Court [to which we have nothing analogous in England] received Judges of a new character appointed by the President from the ranks of freedom, no one can say but that ere long the right to stop the trade would be made good. In the address of South Carolina quoted above, you learn the alarm which the planters justly felt of new blood being poured into the Supreme Court.

Thus the key to the whole political movement was the

possession of the President's Cabinet: for, while this was in the hands of the South, the Executive Administration was purposely abused, Lynch law and every form of violence in favour of slavery was winked at, free speech in the Senate was checked by brutal assault, the slave-trade was left unpunished, the Supreme Court was filled with judges devoted to slavery, and (as the story of Kansas showed) the Federal army itself was made a tool of lawless violence. Both sides therefore betook themselves to the Presidential election as decisive of the struggle.

It is not pretended that the Republican party, which is counted by millions had foresight to look much farther than the first steps of the programme. They felt that it had become absolutely essential to resist the Slave Power and they took their first step resolutely: nevertheless the leaders looked on steadily to an early termination of the system of slavery. Both Mr. Seward, who at first was the leader of the party, and Mr. Lincoln who was finally chosen as candidate for the Presidency, had in distinct terms declared that it was the duty of the North, not only to check and limit slavery by law, but to take measures for its ultimate extinction. It suffices now to quote some of Mr. Seward's public words: "Slavery can be limited to its present bounds, it can be ameliorated; it can be and it must be abolished; you and I can and must do it." The South has not ceased to treat Mr. Seward and Mr. Lincoln as avowed abolitionists; and so they were, though they *intended* to use only legal methods, which would necessarily be indirect and gradual. Is it from ignorance of this, that so many friends of the Northern cause have spoken as if Mr. Lincoln had become an emeny of slavery only by the stress of the war?

But I must add some words in the very singular programme (or platform, as the Americans call it) on which the election was made to turn. The Southerners were firmly convinced (rightly or wrongly) that exclusion from new Territories is to them—not only politically, but—*commercially* ruinous. Seeing all round them the blight of the soil by slavery, and mere wildernesses made where fertility abounded some ten or fifteen years before, they dread to be choked by want of space. So frightful is the picture of desolation, as not only to fill their imaginations, but even to convince Englishmen and Northern visitors that their fears are just. Yet there is simultaneously an opposite statement, namely, the vehement cupidity of the South for more negroes *as a commercial necessity*. If we believe them, they are in danger of having too little land for their negroes and too few negroes for their land. In other words, their craving for wealth and power is insatiable. That is intelligible enough; but commercially it is impossible that each article at once should be in excess, when the ease of migration is so great.

Which of the two then are we to believe to have been relatively excessive? The reply is decisively given by the fact, that the price of negroes has been perpetually rising for the last half century. This proves that less and less want of land is felt, in spite of the natural increase of slaves. Moreover we learn that in Missouri, Arkansas, Texas and Florida the untouched land is still enormous.—I therefore regard the mania for new territories to be commercially a delusion, and believe that either mere ambition or the escape of slaves over the Mexican frontier, not commercial need, prompts the zeal for new areas of cultivation. Nevertheless, the South has nourished this delusion; and the Republican party (wisely, as the event shows) selected the Southern ambition for new land as the point on which the Election should turn. Mr. Lincoln engaged to refuse to permit new Slave States; the Southern candidate engaged to allow them. On this issue Mr. Lincoln was elected by a "fabulous majority." After the secession had commenced and negociation was attempted by Southern advocates who were still outwardly adhering to the Union, we know by information from one of them, Mr. Morehead, ex-Governor of Virginia, that they broke off all conference when Mr. Lincoln positively refused to yield about new Slave States.—Whatever may be said of their *commercial* value, that certainly was only in the distant future. The immediate importance of the point was *political*. With the certainty of having no new Slave States, came the prospect to the South of losing its majority in the senate: hence the secession was finally determined on by the States which hesitated longest.

I think it well here briefly to state the glaring evidence which shows the claim of secession to be illegal, and that the separate States of the Union had ceased to be independent. They had solemnly yielded up every emblem of sovereignty. The forts on their area were all, both constitutionally and in fact, in the hand of the Federal Government, which built, repaired, armed, provisioned, manned and commanded them. It devolved on that Government to defend all the States from foreign attack, and for this purpose it had an absolute right to demand soldiers of each for the protection of all. This one fact is decisive in itself. The Federal Congress had also a right to contract pecuniary engagements in the name of all for the protection of each, and to make treaties with foreign powers, binding on all. No State had a right of alliance or treaty or embassy, or of coining money; nor could any foreign Government (as England) be unaware that the Union was a single Nation; for it had one Flag and one Ambassador to us, and never had been known or recognized by more than one. Internal duties and custom houses were totally forbidden. Moreover, of the seceding States some, not at all the least important, as Louisiana, Arkansas and Missouri, were formed by the Union, on land surrendered to the Union, and paid for by the money of the Union. Others, as Florida and Texas, were conquered by the arms and blood of the Union. The manifestoes of the seceding States are those of insurgents apprehensive of coming unjust rule, not of sovereigns retiring from a league; nor did they appeal to legal processes for separation. As a final comment, their President Buchannan, who had winked at and aided all the treasonable doings, yet made public avowal that secession was illegal, when so to do was to criminate himself in the very crisis of abandoning power.

But with the secession of eight or nine States from the Union the whole controversy was violently altered. *The matters in contest were changed.* The previous question had been : "How to repress, ameliorate and ultimately extinguish slavery by purely Constitutional means ?" To ask that question any longer was absurd, when Constitutional proceedings had been defeated by violence. A new and *far greater* question had arisen: "How to secure that any laws, any constitution whatever, shall have any validity ?" By confounding these two different phases of the struggle, the English press has involved itself in a maze of error, and deceives our nation. The North suddenly found itself in appalling danger. Its arsenals, navy-yards, fortresses, treasuries, had been seized and emptied, its civil and military service disorganized. For those months was deliberate anarchy, while President Buchannan sat idle, and allowed rebellion to run its course. Internal dissolution, perpetual civil war, ruin to material industry, general demoralization, ultimate military tyranny, the fate of Buenos Ayres and Paraguay for another half-century, suddenly threatened the free States. If at that moment

Kentucky, Missouri and Maryland would have renounced slavery, and thus cleared the residual Union from complicity with it, this could not have brought satisfaction to any wise man of the North. To allow success to the perjured office holders who had committed the very worst form of treason, would be a precedent of the most deadly kind;—a precedent which no Power has more reason to deprecate and abhor, than the Queen of England, whose ministers have winked at it, and all but applauded it. Not to repel the principle that any State might secede at pleasure, was to dissolve all coherence in the remnant of the Union; was to permit Maine and Massachusetts to join Canada, Virginia to carry off the Chesapeake to the South, Maryland to claim the Metropolis for herself and the mouths of the Pennsylvanian rivers. The South would inevitably soon have verified the boast of its Vice-President, Alexander Stephens, and have become the Paramount Power of the Continent, by acting on the hopes and fears of the Border States and those of the Upper Mississippi, thus gaining a strong party and drawing them over to itself. No laws for Freedom could have stood firm. The Paramount Power would have swept them away, and have "reconstructed" the Union after its own programme, extending slavery over the nearer States, and expelling New England as fanatical, with barren soil and harsh climate. If the *principle* of secession were once allowed, the sinews of the Union were hamstrung: its treasury was without basis; no creditor of £100 would know what State was his responsible debtor; its political respect and influence would be mortally wounded. To have truckled to the rebels at that moment and yielded any thing to their violence and illegality would have been a fatal policy to the North, ensuring either its early absorption into the Slave Power, or a war vastly worse than the present. Self-defence being thus urgent, no one has or had a right to call upon the North to make any other aim primary at such a time. To complain that she did not make war *for the negro*, and say that "it would have been higher and more generous," is a perfect extravagance: for in no case, and *at no time*, could any one justly claim that she should prefer extra-legal to legal remedies of negro-oppression, and voluntarily rush into the horrible uncertainties and certain miseries of war; still less *then* had she strength to spare. *Nothing carried the North into the war, but the overthrow of Legality.* Her natural and chosen weapons are those proper to human and moral natures: when these are wrested from her, she must needs fight with weapons of war, but only to regain her ravished legal powers. Until Legality and Nationality had been recovered, the Negro question became *secondary*, being superseded by a far more urgent controversy. To the South indeed the object of contest remained as at first. It fought for Slavery, first by the Constitution, next against the Constitution. But the North contended, in peace against Slavery, by the Constitution; in war, of necessity, for the Constitution itself; as the pledge and means of Order, Civilization, Right, Freedom and Humanity.

It has here been shown how entirely *illegal* was the secession of the South: but mere illegality was the smallest part of the guilt. The great and horrible guilt lay in *the end avowedly sought*,—the perpetuation of that wickedest form of slavery ever known,—a slavery against which English peeresses in 1854 uttered their anguish to the wide world. The anarchical, immoral and inhuman doctrine is now preached to us—*by Conservatives !*—that because the insurgents are said to be five millions, they have a natural right of insurrection, without moral grievances except the fear of being forced to abandon slavery: and we are to take for granted the real unanimity of the five millions, none of whom have had freedom of speech or of voting.

One of our Cabinet Ministers is reported to have said publicly, that *our great fear* in England was, lest, *if* the South should offer to return to the Union, President Lincoln should make peace without securing freedom to the negro. Many less eminent have said the same thing and have treated attachment to the Union as equivalent to hypocrisy and treachery. Is this because they ardently wish for its break-up ? The cry against the President as *self-condemned* for declaring that he is at war for the Union and for the Union alone, has rung from end to end of the country and has met one in every drawing-room, displaying qualities of mind in the English gentry, which I decline here to characterize.

The very reasoners who whimper about a fratricidal war, when their duty is to condemn an atrocious conspiracy of ruffianism, which their sympathy has encouraged and in many cases—legally and illegally—their wealth has armed ; these same reasoners have called on us to degrade President Lincoln in our estimate to the level of those ruffians for being willing to accept peace at the earliest moment at which he could honorably obtain the ends *for which alone* the war had been entered. Whoever needlessly prolongs a war for an end foreign to the original quarrel, does nearly the same as plunge into a new war ; and if Philanthropy was no adequate cause for forcing the the war originally, it is a most doubtful justification for forcing the prolongation of a war. He who volunteers the prolongation, does so at tremendous risk. He will generally discontent his own side, and make the enemy more obstinate. This, which is a general probability, was in Mr. Lincoln's case a certainty ; for the Democratic Party and the Border States would have been enraged by it. The very fact is made a reproach by his English

assailants,—and by friends of the slave, forsooth! whereas
it is one of his obvious justifications. It would have been
highly criminal if he had risked miscarriage in the object
of the war,—vindication of Law against violence and
treason,—by refusing to accept an honorable peace and
thus alienating a large part of his supporters. This is
what his English enemies have blandly or insolently
demanded.

But what would have happened so terrible to the
negro, if the South—suppose last May, when disheartened
by the great career of Northern successes,—had come
back into the Union on its old footing without concessions
from the North? That the North might justly claim
guarantees against renewed treason and exclusion of traitors
from power, of course I am not denying. But in every
case all the hopes formed by the " Republican " Party—
that is, by Mr. Lincoln's party,—would have been brighter
than before the abortive secession. In the interval they
had freed Columbia, the district of the Capitol,—had
pronounced the Territories (*i.e.* the areas which as yet
had no State Organization) sacred to liberty, and had
made important treaties; none of which things could
have been done so speedily, but for the absence of
Southern members from Congress. Thus the party of
Freedom had gained at once objects which might otherwise have cost the struggle of years; and the Southerners
in their return would have found themselves to their
chagrin to be sitting on free soil in the Capitol,—an event
which they had in prospect denounced as so unendurable
that it would alone justify secession. Moreover, an
immense result had been won by the alienation of the
Northern " Democratic " party from them. For,--let
the leaders of that party struggle as they may to regain
their old importance, yet nothing can restore to the party
its old numbers. Myriads of it resented the attempt of

the South to break in pieces that idol of the "Democrats," the mighty Union, and meanwhile the party of Freedom had been consolidated. Thus all chance had vanished that any coming Presidential Election would fall on a candidate bound over to Southern interests. In consequence the real Peace-men, Mr. Lincoln's friends, would be able more boldly than ever to devote themselves to bring about by law and by the pleadings of justice and true interest a gradual emancipation. Nor only so ; but it was within possibility that the President might *in the cause of humanity* interfere against the Inter-State slave-trade. Nothing could hinder this, after the South had vainly tried to secede, if the Congress did not actively thwart him. When once the fortresses of the South were won or given back, its armies disbanded, and the whole force of the Union again in the President's hand, the slave-holders would have to resist in Congress as best they might; but would have had no chance by recurring to the game of secession, if disgusted with Congress. But in fact, all these certain disadvantages from Reunion are the very cause which has made the South implacable.

When Mr. Lincoln did come to the conviction, that "for military reasons" he not only *might* prudently, but *must*, pronounce the negroes in the rebellious States legally free; I certainly wish that he had enunciated it on the Hon. Charles Sumner's principle,—that slavery, being a mere local enactment, falls away of itself in a State, which, by disowning the Federal Government, forfeits its own claim to have its local laws recognized. It is doubly clear, that thenceforward the Federal Executive can know no distinction of men on the rebel area, except that of loyal and disloyal persons. I say, it is doubly clear : for even on an earlier occasion of war [War of Florida, 1836] when there was no rebellion, the principle was acted on under Southern Presidents, that the Federal army-officers know no distinction of slave and free, since they are not bound to be acquainted with the local laws. Nothing is more obvious, than that in a time of rebellion the President has a *natural* and *necessary* right to summon to his standard all the loyal subjects of the Union without distinction of colour. It is not as slaves, but as loyalists that he knows the negroes. By being silent on this argument, Mr. Lincoln has allowed his opponents to pretend that he is acting against a power which is legitimately foreign to him, and is taking away its subjects for his warlike convenience ; as did the Russians [early in the Crimean war] in Moldavia and Wallachia, not without grave and just rebuke.

What results from this struggle are we now to expect ? I am not about to attempt speculation on military details, but I shall recapitulate in summary the progress of the war hitherto [* * * *]. From such a comparison of eighteen months the inevitable result seems to be,—*unless warships from England derange events*,—an absolute conquest by the North.

But I am told, the great and insoluble question remains : How will the North be able to *govern* the South, if victorious ? This question seems to afflict with great anxiety Englishmen who did not trouble their heads to ask, how England was to govern India, after blowing Hindoos from the cannon's mouth to prevent the possibility of burying them ;—after polluting Brahmins with blood before hanging them ;—after studying to make their kinsfolk believe that our generals had deprived their victims of all hope of a happy hereafter. I have never heard that Earl Derby nor yet Earl Russell, avowed to the world any misgiving as to our power of governing Oudh, when Lord Dalhousie annexed it under false pretexts, repudiated the English debt to the king, seized all the king's private property, down to his jewels, wardrobe, library and furniture; drove all the nobility by their very patriotism to submit to ejection from the high civil and military service, hereby reducing thousands to beggary; or when afterwards, barely in order to reclaim its own, this province rebelled, we reconquered Lucknow with unspeakable horrors, reducing the finest parts of that beautiful city to "a pestilential heap;" and this, though the resistance was truly national,—the Court, the Nobles and the Peasants being all intensely united against us. Nor do I remember that either Whigs or Tories were made anxious as to our future, when English fleets and armies rent away all Pegu from the king of Burma, on pretexts lighter than in any war of conquest since the Pope has left off giving away the kingdoms of the heathen. The men, who, if they did not swell the howl of vengeance against innocent Indians, yet made no protests against hangings of men by the score and burning of houses to drive out fugitive mutineers,—these same men loudly proclaim in Parliament their distress and horror that General Butler should use a harsh word against the insolence of Southern women, who are eager partizans of a slavery reeking with rape and incest. Such being the prevalent tone of sentiment among English public men, I for my part draw a sponge over all that they have said concerning the American future, and study it from my own point of view.

A rotten tyranny is like a cone poised on its sharp end. Once overturned it never can be set up again. We all know it in the case of the Spanish Colonies, Naples, North Italy. We do not fear that a great Poland or Hungary once free would be reconquered. But of all tyrannies the most rotten is that of oligarchical slave-holders. Once set the slaves of the South free, *arm* them and *organize* them; and it is certain that the Slave Power is for ever killed. This would be true, even if the Southern Confederacy had the rank and composition of a nation : but it has not.   It has no past history, no noble memories to kindle it : shame on the ignorance which had compared it to Hungary ! - no cohesion of Orders, no middle class.   It consists virtually of a few slave-holding families, perhaps in all a thirtieth part of the population; with a great mass of despised poor whites, and by their side the three millions of slaves. All the *interests* of the poorer whites lie with the North. The most effective treatise against slavery in modern days,—if Mrs. Stowe's "Uncle Tom" is to be excepted,— is the work on the last Census by Mr. Helper, himself a portionless white of the South.   Experience agrees with the prediction that contact with the Northerners must rapidly convert this class of white men to the cause of freedom.   What they can do in that cause, appeared first in Missouri, after the violences in Kansas.   We have since seen how they came over in Maryland, in North Carolina, even in New Orleans; nor is the account from Pensacola different.   In Alabama they have of late been enduring a martyrdom.   In North Carolina they have fought bravely for the Union : in New Orleans they have gladly taken military service.   Maryland seems to have been made substantially Unionist by two years' Northern occupation, though at Mr. Lincoln's accession to power the hostile faction was predominant : indeed until last autumn the Southerners fondly believed they had only to march in, and would be welcomed.   The more the poor whites have been deceived in this war, the quicker, after once they are defeated, is their conversion likely to be.   And in the cause of humanity (even if there were no slaves) they need to be disarmed, that the horrible assassinations and lynch law and daily frays may be put down.   Our experience of Ireland tells us, how effective registration of arms may be made.   If negroes and other loyalists were cautiously armed and the unloyal disarmed, it scarcely would need the influx of the Northern settlers to keep the peace. Perhaps, the soldiers of the Union will colonize the South largely: black regiments ought to hold the fortresses of the South.

But with the positive overthrow of slavery not only are the slave-oligarchy made helpless; they also lose all motive for attempting new rebellion. Messrs. Lindsay, Laird and Zachary Pearson will not lavish effort upon them again. Their guilty phantasy of a vast Slave Empire being once dispelled, would they risk life and fortune for the chance of becoming a petty independency? What bait could they offer to the white millions, when once freedom of speech and press had pervaded the South? New deception would be impossible. What chance of secret conspiracy, when the free negroes are all eyes and ears to watch against it? Once totally beaten in this war and forced to submit absolutely to freedom, the families of the planters would soon be reconciled, by despair of their old dream, to the not very hard fate of being honorable citizens in the greatest and noblest of republics.

Of course I do not pretend that all difficulties will vanish in a year; but in great events nothing but a choice of difficulties is proposed. This also I will say:— The longer and the harder the Confederates struggle, the less power of after-resistance will they leave to themselves; and *as far as they are concerned*, the easier will be the task to the North, after once the victory is won. It is *not* from the now rebellious Confederates that I expect the main *ultimate* difficulties, *but* from the States still loyal, which cling to the love of slavery and proud contempt of coloured men. All experience of history, and all indications of the present, suggest, that a new and perplexing contest may flame out among the victors, the moment that complete and irreversible victory is attained. But with three million blacks free and loyal, there will be no graver danger than such as besets Free States from ordinary civil faction.

I cannot know what measures President Lincoln may think needful. I *hope* he will understand that to háve a vast body of *black freeholders* is of prime importance in the future of the Union. But of one thing I am sure :— that English politicians need not distress their hearts with these foreign cares. They have yet Ireland to look after, and perhaps will not be pleased to have advice about it from America.

Nevertheless, it is a question of humanity, of Internationalism, and therefore a question for England, whether the North is to allow *a little* South to become independent and sustain slavery. If the North were disposed to this, the folly of the deed would seem to me to be on the scale of a crime; for the watching against border-war would be a permanent burden greater than the task of completing the conquest. To leave the germ of independent slavery is to ensure the renewal of convulsion. But besides this, NOW on the ground of HONOR the North cannot leave its work thus incomplete. The President has declared the slaves of the rebels free: Congress has confirmed his proclamation. Thus they are recognized beyond dispute as citizens, free as well as loyal. They clearly have a right to protection. *This was always true;* but neither the Executive nor the Legislature can any longer deny it. *To abandon them* permanently to a foreign and oppressive power, unless under the stress of an overwhelming force and absolute exhaustion,* would be now a treachery. If any thing could be likely to precipitate a servile war of the worst

---

* P.S., 1889.—Alas! it has been done, in despite of martyred Abolitionists.

kind, it would be such a sudden disappointment of hope.
Thus, even if I did not know how the conquest was
afterwards to be held, yet if I saw the least symptom of
faltering, I would urge the North to persevere by a topic
which alas! it was impossible to use for our conquest of
Oudh, "*Be just and fear not!* you are now pledged to
set the oppressed free and break every yoke. Break it,
in the name of God! and end these accursed inhumanities
with their unspeakable impurities and the contagion of
wickedness which they spread to mercantile Europe."
And as regards the white men of the South themselves,
bravely says the wise Mrs. Beecher Stowe: "The children of our conquered assailants will rise up and call us
blessed."